OPPOSING
VIEWPOINTS®
SERIES

High School
Alternative Programs

Other Books of Related Interest:

Opposing Viewpoints Series

Charter Schools

Education

School Reform

At Issue Series

High School Dropouts

Should Junk Food Be Sold in School?

What Is the Future of Higher Education?

Current Controversies Series

College Admissions

"Congress shall make
no law . . . abridging
the freedom of speech,
or of the press."

First Amendment to the US Constitution

The basic foundation of our democracy is the First Amendment guarantee of freedom of expression. The Opposing Viewpoints series is dedicated to the concept of this basic freedom and the idea that it is more important to practice it than to enshrine it.

OPPOSING
VIEWPOINTS®
SERIES

High School Alternative Programs

Noah Berlatsky, Book Editor

GREENHAVEN PRESS
A part of Gale, Cengage Learning

GALE
CENGAGE Learning®

Farmington Hills, Mich • San Francisco • New York • Waterville, Maine
Meriden, Conn • Mason, Ohio • Chicago

Elizabeth Des Chenes, *Director, Content Strategy*
Douglas Dentino, *Manager, New Product*

© 2015 Greenhaven Press, a part of Gale, Cengage Learning.

WCN: 01-100-101

Gale and Greenhaven Press are registered trademarks used herein under license.

For more information, contact:
Greenhaven Press
27500 Drake Rd.
Farmington Hills, MI 48331-3535
Or you can visit our Internet site at gale.cengage.com

For product information and technology assistance, contact us at

Gale Customer Support, 1-800-877-4253
For permission to use material from this text or product, submit all requests online at
www.cengage.com/permissions

Further permissions questions can be emailed to permissionrequest@cengage.com

Articles in Greenhaven Press anthologies are often edited for length to meet page requirements. In addition, original titles of these works are changed to clearly present the main thesis and to explicitly indicate the author's opinion. Every effort is made to ensure that Greenhaven Press accurately reflects the original intent of the authors. Every effort has been made to trace the owners of copyrighted material.

Cover Image copyright ©jocic/Shutterstock.com.

LIBRARY OF CONGRESS CATALOGING-IN-PUBLICATION DATA

High School Alternative Programs / Noah Berlatsky, book editor.
    pages cm. -- -- (Opposing Viewpoints) "Opposing Viewpoints: High School Alternative Programs: Opposing Viewpoints is the leading source for libraries and classrooms in need of current-issue materials. The viewpoints are selected from a wide range of highly respected sources and publications"-- Provided by publisher.
    Includes bibliographical references and index.
    ISBN 978-0-7377-7270-8 (hardback) -- ISBN 978-0-7377-7271-5 (paperback)
    1. Alternative education. 2. High schools--United States. 3. Education, Secondary--United States. I. Berlatsky, Noah, editor of compilation.
    LC46.4.H54 2014
    371.04--dc23
                                                                    2014018239

Printed in the United States of America
1 2 3 4 5 6 7 18 17 16 15 14

Contents

Chapter 4: Is Online Learning a Good Alternative for High School Students?

Why Consider Opposing Viewpoints?

> *"The only way in which a human being can make some approach to knowing the whole of a subject is by hearing what can be said about it by persons of every variety of opinion and studying all modes in which it can be looked at by every character of mind. No wise man ever acquired his wisdom in any mode but this."*
>
> *John Stuart Mill*

In our media-intensive culture it is not difficult to find differing opinions. Thousands of newspapers and magazines and dozens of radio and television talk shows resound with differing points of view. The difficulty lies in deciding which opinion to agree with and which "experts" seem the most credible. The more inundated we become with differing opinions and claims, the more essential it is to hone critical reading and thinking skills to evaluate these ideas. Opposing Viewpoints books address this problem directly by presenting stimulating debates that can be used to enhance and teach these skills. The varied opinions contained in each book examine many different aspects of a single issue. While examining these conveniently edited opposing views, readers can develop critical thinking skills such as the ability to compare and contrast authors' credibility, facts, argumentation styles, use of persuasive techniques, and other stylistic tools. In short, the Opposing Viewpoints Series is an ideal way to attain the higher-level thinking and reading skills so essential in a culture of diverse and contradictory opinions.

In addition to providing a tool for critical thinking, Opposing Viewpoints books challenge readers to question their own strongly held opinions and assumptions. Most people form their opinions on the basis of upbringing, peer pressure, and personal, cultural, or professional bias. By reading carefully balanced opposing views, readers must directly confront new ideas as well as the opinions of those with whom they disagree. This is not to argue simplistically that everyone who reads opposing views will—or should—change his or her opinion. Instead, the series enhances readers' understanding of their own views by encouraging confrontation with opposing ideas. Careful examination of others' views can lead to the readers' understanding of the logical inconsistencies in their own opinions, perspective on why they hold an opinion, and the consideration of the possibility that their opinion requires further evaluation.

Evaluating Other Opinions

To ensure that this type of examination occurs, Opposing Viewpoints books present all types of opinions. Prominent spokespeople on different sides of each issue as well as well-known professionals from many disciplines challenge the reader. An additional goal of the series is to provide a forum for other, less known, or even unpopular viewpoints. The opinion of an ordinary person who has had to make the decision to cut off life support from a terminally ill relative, for example, may be just as valuable and provide just as much insight as a medical ethicist's professional opinion. The editors have two additional purposes in including these less known views. One, the editors encourage readers to respect others' opinions—even when not enhanced by professional credibility. It is only by reading or listening to and objectively evaluating others' ideas that one can determine whether they are worthy of consideration. Two, the inclusion of such viewpoints encourages the important critical thinking skill of objectively evaluating an author's credentials and bias. This evaluation will illuminate an author's reasons for taking a particular stance on an issue and will aid in readers' evaluation of the author's ideas.

It is our hope that these books will give readers a deeper understanding of the issues debated and an appreciation of the complexity of even seemingly simple issues when good and honest people disagree. This awareness is particularly important in a democratic society such as ours in which people enter into public debate to determine the common good. Those with whom one disagrees should not be regarded as enemies but rather as people whose views deserve careful examination and may shed light on one's own.

Thomas Jefferson once said that "difference of opinion leads to inquiry, and inquiry to truth." Jefferson, a broadly educated man, argued that "if a nation expects to be ignorant and free . . . it expects what never was and never will be." As individuals and as a nation, it is imperative that we consider the opinions of others and examine them with skill and discernment. The Opposing Viewpoints series is intended to help readers achieve this goal.

David L. Bender and Bruno Leone,
Founders

Introduction

> *"My husband and I both attended public schools. We believe in the benefits, both individual and communal, of supporting public schools. We hate the idea of paying more for our kids to attend elementary school than I paid for either my bachelor's or master's degrees. We hate that we were sending our kids to a school at which others (friends, neighbors, acquaintances) are excluded by the 'inadequacy' of their incomes. . . . But despite all our guilt and discomfort and high ideals, we came to the decision that we weren't sending our children to Chicago's public schools."*
>
> —Kim Brooks,
> *"My Private School Guilt,"*
> Salon, *October 8, 2012*

One of the main alternatives to a public high school education in the United States is private school. Jack Jennings writing in a March 28, 2013, article at the *Huffington Post* says approximately 10 percent of US secondary students were enrolled in a private high school in 2009, the most recent year for which data are available. Catholic schools are by far the largest segment of private school enrollment, making up fully three-quarters of all private high school enrollment. They are followed in popularity by nonsectarian schools, which account for one-eighth of secondary school enrollment and one-third of combined elementary and secondary school enrollment.

Although they make up a fairly small proportion of overall students, private schools have often been the focus of controversy. For example, in an August 29, 2013, article at *Slate*, Allison Benedikt states,

> I am not an education policy wonk: I'm just judgmental. But it seems to me that if every single parent sent every single child to public school, public schools would improve. This would not happen immediately. It could take generations. Your children and grandchildren might get mediocre educations in the meantime, but it will be worth it, for the eventual common good.

In other words, Benedikt believes that when people with money and resources leave the public schools for private schools, the public schools suffer. "Everyone," she says, "needs to be invested in our public schools in order for them to get better." She argues that studies show that the major determinant of student outcomes is family background, not private or public school. Affluent families therefore do not need private schools for their children to succeed. However, public schools need affluent families if they are going to prosper. She concludes, "Use the energy you have otherwise directed at fighting to get your daughter a slot at the competitive private school to fight for more computers at the public school. Use your connections to power and money and innovation to make your local school—the one you are now sending your child to—better."

Benedikt's article prompted numerous responses and objections. An August 30, 2013, article at Minutemen.com argues that Benedikt is promoting an immoral ideology in which "children belong to the state and should be sacrificed for the greater good." Emily Willingham, in an August 29, 2013, article at *Forbes*, argues that there is little research to suggest that wealthy students attending public schools would necessarily improve those schools. She writes,

Where studies find that money—referencing public funds—affects outcomes, they also find that teacher pay, ability, education, and experience are also profoundly important. Adult educational and cultural role models and people who care about a student individually are also deeply influential. Nary a word about presence of rich people.

Along similar lines, Ben Adler in a September 3, 2013, article in the *Atlantic* argues that affluent people attending public school would not have much influence on school quality because wealthy people live near wealthy public schools. In other words, Adler argues, when people in wealthy suburbs attend their local public school, that has little beneficial impact on inner-city public schools in low-income areas. Adler adds that eliminating all private schools would simply lead to more wealthy people moving into wealthy, often suburban, school districts, which would have no beneficial effect on the most resource-starved public schools.

The argument around Benedikt's article focuses on wealthy parents, but other families also send their children to private school. Jason Bedrick, in a November 13, 2013, report at the Cato Institute website, discusses a report that surveyed parents of low- and middle-income families as to why they had chosen private schools. Bedrick quotes the report as follows:

> The top five reasons why parents chose a private school for their children are all related to school climate and classroom management, including "better student discipline" (50.9 percent), "better learning environment" (50.8 percent), "smaller class sizes" (48.9 percent), "improved student safety" (46.8 percent), and "more individual attention for my child" (39.3 percent).

Interestingly, school test scores were not a high priority for most parents. More than 98 percent of these parents were satisfied or very satisfied with their private school decision.

The remainder of *Opposing Viewpoints: High School Alternative Programs* looks at other controversies and viewpoints pertaining to alternative high school programs and choices. Individual chapters focus on the questions "Can Alternative Programs Help At-Risk and Special-Needs Students?," "What Are Alternatives to a High School Diploma?," "Are Charter and Magnet Schools Good Alternatives for Students?," and "Is On-line Learning a Good Alternative for High School Students?" After completing the volume, readers will have the tools needed to evaluate a range of high school alternatives and make informed decisions about the worth of such programs.

**OPPOSING
VIEWPOINTS®
SERIES**

CHAPTER 1

Can Alternative Programs Help At-Risk and Special-Needs Students?

Chapter Preface

Should blind students be included in mainstream class-rooms, or should they attend special schools that directly address their needs? Are there other possible options? In general, parents and educators have tended to think that blind children should be included in mainstream classrooms. "Educators of blind and visually impaired children have believed since the turn of the century that there is a place in the public schools for their students," explain S.A. Curry and P.H. Hatlen in an article at *Expanded Core Curriculum Advocacy*. Curry and Hatlen, however, argue that by the mid-1970s some serious problems with mainstream education had become apparent. Many blind students who had been educated in mainstream environments did not develop academic skills and had trouble in social/emotional areas as well. As a result, Curry and Hatlen conclude that educators should put less emphasis on trying to put blind children in mainstream classrooms and more on finding the most appropriate placement for each student, whether that placement is in a mainstream classroom or in an alternative program.

In the book *Psycho-Social Dynamics of Blind Students* published in 2011, Ranjita Dawn talked to blind students in both mainstream and alternative settings. Blind students in alternative schools said that "the homogenous setting made it easier for them to relate well with others having similar problems and needs." They also said that they received "more individualized attention," which "encouraged them towards independent thinking." On the other hand, blind students in mainstream settings stressed that their placement with sighted students provided an opportunity for them to develop greater communication and academic skills. They also felt that they were better able to assess their overall performance through comparison with their sighted classmates.

There can, then, be advantages and disadvantages both to integrating blind students in mainstream classrooms and to putting blind students in a special program. There are also mixed possibilities, in which students spend most or part of their day in a general classroom and then have special classes in which teachers focus on their individual needs. Given the range of options, parents, schools, and students need to look at each individual situation and determine what education format is best for each student.

The remainder of this chapter looks at possible options available to students with other special needs, such as hearing impairment and mental disabilities. As with blind students, options for other special-needs students include integration into mainstream classrooms, special alternative programs and schools, or a mix of both approaches.

> *"An examination of the dropout-prevention interventions that show measurable results shines some light on what it likely takes to reduce a student's chance of dropping out."*

Alternative High School Programs Can Help Address Dropout Rates

John H. Tyler and Magnus Lofstrom

John H. Tyler is an associate professor of education at Brown University; Magnus Lofstrom is a research fellow at the Public Policy Institute of California. In the following viewpoint, the authors look at alternative high school programs that attempt to lower dropout rates. They conclude that many popular programs do not in fact lower rates. However, some programs have been successful. These programs focus on such factors as close mentoring and monitoring of students, as well as family outreach, to deal with students' out-of-school challenges.

John H. Tyler and Magnus Lofstrom, "Finishing High School: Alternative Pathways and Dropout Recovery," *Future of Children*, vol. 19, no. 1, Spring 2009, pp. 88–93. Copyright © 2009 by Princeton University. All rights reserved. From *The Future of Children*, a collaboration of the Woodrow Wilson School of Public and International Affairs at Princeton University and the Brookings Institution.

As you read, consider the following questions:

1. What are the key features of a career academy model, according to the authors?

2. What is the added cost per year per student at talent development high schools?

3. What is the Quantum Opportunity Program, and how do the authors rate its effectiveness?

The high costs associated with dropping out make clear the need for programs to help students stay in school. The [National] Dropout Prevention Center/Network lists hundreds of dropout-prevention programs in its online database of "model programs." Only relatively few of these programs, however, have been rigorously evaluated for effectiveness. Even fewer have proved effective in achieving this goal. As Mark Dynarski and Philip Gleason write in a report on dropout-prevention programs, "Dropping out is as hard to prevent as it is easy to do." Based on the evidence, one might add that it is equally hard to identify confidently the programs that are effective.

Dropout-Prevention Interventions

In what follows, we group dropout-prevention interventions into two categories. The first is interventions that set dropout prevention as the primary goal and that target specific students or groups of students. The second is interventions that have a broader goal than dropout prevention and a broader target audience than "at-risk" students, but that, nevertheless, aim to lower dropout rates. The first category embraces programs in the regular school or in the community, alternative schools for at-risk students, and smaller learning communities that tend to fit the "school-within-a-school" model and that target at-risk students. The second, broader category includes school restructuring or school reform models. Broadly stated, programs in both categories aim to lower dropout rates through one or more of four mechanisms: increasing school attendance, increasing student school engagement and learning, building student self-esteem, and helping students cope with the challenges and problems that contribute to the likelihood of dropping out.

To date, relatively few evaluations of dropout-prevention interventions could be considered rigorous. One of the largest rigorously conducted evaluations was a late-1990s study of twenty-one different interventions, each funded by the U.S. Department of Education's School Dropout Demonstration Assistance Program (SDDAP). In addition to the SDDAP evaluations, a second source of evidence on the efficacy of dropout-prevention interventions can be found in the Department of Education's What Works Clearinghouse (WWC), which reviews and synthesizes studies of a wide variety of education interventions. The combined findings of the SDDAP evaluation and the WWC synthesis of dropout-prevention programs leave one less than sanguine about the knowledge base about how to lower dropout rates.

What Works

The SDDAP evaluation, conducted by Mathematica Policy Research Inc., included both targeted and broadly defined dropout-prevention efforts. Targeted interventions were usually evaluated through randomized, controlled experiments, while the evaluations of the school-restructuring efforts were quasi-experimental and used observationally similar schools as the comparison group for SDDAP schools. The evaluation looked at sixteen targeted interventions and five school-restructuring projects. Eight of the interventions took place at the middle school level. Two of the targeted interventions at the high school level were community-based programs aimed at helping students who had already left school acquire a GED [general equivalency diploma].

The key finding from the SDDAP evaluations is that "most programs made almost no difference in preventing dropping out *in general*." Some SDDAP programs did make a difference on some outcomes, and we will take a closer look at one of the more successful programs. One of the more consistent positive findings in the SDDAP evaluations, however, involves programs to increase GED acquisition among students who have already left school. Although increasing the GED attainment rate of school dropouts may be a laudable outcome, it seems less clear that it should be considered as successful dropout *prevention*.

The picture is hardly any brighter when it comes to findings of the What Works Clearinghouse. To date, the first-wave WWC review of dropout-prevention programs has looked at fifty-nine studies of sixteen programs. From this group, ten of the programs had undergone evaluations that were rigorous enough to make it possible to reach firm conclusions about program effectiveness. These ten programs include a wide range of interventions: counseling and monitoring, school restructuring and curriculum redesign, financial incentives for students and families, and community services designed to mitigate factors that can negatively affect school achievement and success.

Of the ten programs, five showed promise in reducing dropout rates. Two of the five—Achievement for Latinos through Academic Success (ALAS) and High School Redirection—are no longer active. ALAS, a pilot program launched in San Diego during the early 1990s, was designed to address student, school, family, and community factors that affect dropping out. At the end of the ninth grade, 98 percent of the students who were randomly assigned to the ALAS program were still enrolled, compared with 83 percent of the students in the non-ALAS control group. Meanwhile, three years after random assignment, 43 percent of the students assigned to the High School Redirection program—an alternative high school program for students considered at risk—had dropped out, compared with 53 percent of the randomly assigned control group.

The three remaining positive programs represent three distinct approaches to dropout prevention. One, Check & Connect, is a relatively intensive program for (mostly) high school students; a second, career academies, fits the school-within-a-school model; a third, talent development high schools, is best described as whole-school reform. We discuss each in turn.

A Dropout-Prevention Program: Check & Connect

The Check & Connect model, developed through a partner-ship between the University of Minnesota, local public schools, and local community service organizations, was originally funded by the Department of Education. The Check & Connect model "was initially developed for urban middle school students with learning and behavioral challenges and was designed to promote students' engagement with school and learning, and to reduce and prevent dropping out. The model is currently being replicated and field-tested for youth with and without disabilities in grades K–12 in urban and suburban communities." Broadly speaking, Check & Connect works with and coordinates services among the student, family, school, and community to help the student succeed and stay in school.

The signature feature of Check & Connect is the assignment of a "monitor" to each student in the program to be the student's mentor and case worker. In the Check component, the monitor continually assesses the student's school performance, including attendance, behavior, and academics. Monitors are trained to follow up quickly at the first sign that a student is struggling in any of these areas. The Connect component combines individualized attention to the student with the coordination of services and information about the student across school personnel, family, and community service providers. The program carries a minimum two-year commitment to students and families, including the promise and ability to follow highly mobile youth from school to school so that students do not lose services when they move from their original program site.

In two separate experimental evaluations, Check & Connect showed positive effects on staying in school and progressing through school. One study showed that ninth-grade students enrolled in Check & Connect were substantially less likely than control group members to have dropped out of school by the end of the year—9 percent compared with 30 percent. Another study showed that by the expected graduation year, 39 percent of students in the Check & Connect treatment group had dropped out of school compared with 58 percent of the control group. The high dropout rate associated with both groups indicates the level of dropout risk present in the population targeted by Check & Connect. The cost of implementing the Check & Connect model was about $1,400 per student during the 2001–02 school year.

The School-Within-a-School Model: Career Academies

Career academies are another intervention that rigorous evidence shows effective in lowering dropout rates, at least for students most at risk of dropping out. The career academy model has three key features. First, it is organized as a school within a school: students in a smaller and more personal learning atmosphere stay with the same teachers over the three or four years of high school. Second, it includes both academic and vocational course work, with the two integrated in the curriculum and in pedagogy. And, third, it uses partnerships between the academy and local employers to build links between school and work and to provide students with career and work-based learning opportunities.

Begun in the 1970s, the career academy model has both evolved in concept and grown in numbers over time. Today some 1,500 career academies nationwide serve a much wider set of students than the "vocational ed" students who were seen as the original constituents of the academies.

The most important study of career academies is an experimental evaluation of more than 1,700 students who applied for admission to one of nine career academies across the nation. The study found that among high-risk youth, the career academies reduced the baseline dropout rate of 32 percent by 11 percentage points and that in the students' projected twelfth-grade year, 40 percent of the high-risk academy students had earned enough credits to graduate compared with only 26 percent of the high-risk students in the control group. The best cost estimates are that in 2004 the per-pupil cost of educating a student in a career academy was $600 more than the average per-pupil cost of non-academy students.

High School Reform Models: Talent Development High Schools

High school reform models do not usually state "dropout prevention" as the sole objective for school restructuring. Nevertheless, these reform models often have goals related to dropout prevention, in particular increasing students' school engagement and academic achievement. Common components of many reform models include: reorganizing schools into smaller "learning communities"; focusing instruction and curricula on careers or on intensive or high-level English and math instruction, or both; increasing family involvement; and sometimes focusing on a college preparatory curriculum for everyone.

Check & Connect and Student Mental Health

Students who do not feel connected to school or to other people are at risk for a host of mental health problems, including suicidal behavior, and are at increased risk for dropping out of school entirely. . . . At-risk students may require more intensive interventions designed to foster positive relationships and connectedness. A focus on creating school climates that students experience as caring and supportive is a common component of interventions designed to decrease school dropouts and increase school connectedness.

One intervention that has been successfully used to forge stronger and more positive connections between students and school is Check & Connect. This intervention is designed to promote engagement with school and with learning. Students receiving the intervention are assigned a mentor from the school staff who monitors the student, routinely "checks in" with him or her, and helps the student with any problems that might develop. Mentors work to create a relationship with students characterized by mutual trust and open communication. Mentors make a commitment to work with students in Check & Connect for at least 2 years, which emphasizes to students the school personnel's commitment to their development. They also help students become solution-focused and teach them conflict-resolution skills. The program also provides more intensive services if necessary, including increased academic interventions and greater student participation in extracurricular activities.

David N. Miller, Child and Adolescent Suicidal Behavior: School-Based Prevention, Assessment, and Intervention. *New York: Guilford Press, 2010, p. 103.*

Many different reform models have been tried over the years, most without rigorous evidence of success. One exception is talent development high schools (TDHS), a reform model for large high schools that face persistent problems with student attendance, behavior, performance, and dropout rates. The model, developed at Johns Hopkins University, calls for schools to reorganize into small learning communities that feature a curriculum designed to prepare all students for high-level English and math courses, along with measures to increase parent and community involvement in the school. Begun as a partnership between Johns Hopkins and a high school in Baltimore, the TDHS program now includes schools in forty-three districts in fifteen states across the nation. The added cost is about $350 per student per year.

A research design that followed twenty cohorts of ninth graders for up to four years in high school in Philadelphia found that 68 percent of the students in TDHS schools were promoted to tenth grade compared with 60 percent of the comparison group. These positive TDHS findings are notable as it has been hard for high school restructuring efforts to document positive results on outcomes of interest, including keeping students in school. At the same time, the findings should probably be viewed with some caution because they are based on a quasi-experimental research design.

Other Programs

As noted, there are many, many dropout-prevention programs, most of which are "stand alone" programs and many of which are much larger than either ALAS or Check & Connect. As examples, the Valued Youth Program served 108 schools in twenty-four cities in the United States and Brazil during 2002–03, along with an unknown number of schools in Great Britain; the Teen Outreach Program served more than 13,000 students across sixteen states during the 2001–02 school year. These and other larger-scale programs, however, have not been rigorously evaluated, and thus in spite of their apparent popularity, their effectiveness in reducing dropout rates remains unknown.

One program that has been rigorously evaluated through random assignment is the Quantum Opportunity Program (QOP). An intensive and relatively expensive program that offers comprehensive services that begin in the ninth grade, QOP can last for up to five years, providing services even after a student drops out. In six of seven QOP demonstration sites, the cost of the program ranged from $22,000 to $28,000 per enrollee (in 2006 dollars) over the full five years of the demonstration, and labor costs in another QOP demonstration site made the program there even more expensive. In spite of the high costs and intensive nature of the QOP model, experimental evaluations do not offer evidence that QOP participants were more likely to advance in or complete school than were the control group non-participants. These examples suggest that one cannot use a program's popularity or size, cost, or even intensity as evidence of effectiveness.

What It Takes to Prevent Dropping Out

An examination of the dropout-prevention interventions that show measurable results shines some light on what it likely takes to reduce a student's chance of dropping out. Successful programs have some or most of five elements in common. The first element is close mentoring and monitoring of students. With restructuring models, this mentoring occurs as part of the movement to smaller schools or to school-within-a-school models. The normally high adult-student ratio in a smaller learning environment would have to be higher still to reach the level of monitoring found, for example, in Check & Connect. In the High School Redirection model, teachers are encouraged to serve as mentors as well as instructors, and classes are kept small to foster high levels of individual attention. The second element is case management of individual students. Again, case management is most likely to happen in a restructuring model with a movement to a smaller learning community. The remaining three elements are family outreach; curricular reforms that focus either on a career-oriented or experiential approach or an emphasis on gaining proficiency in English and math, or both; and attention to a student's out-of-school problems that can affect attendance, behavior, and performance.

In closing, we note one complication in designing and implementing dropout-prevention programs. Namely, although common risk factors are important in helping to identify potential dropouts, they are relatively inefficient predictors of who will in fact drop out. For example, the risk factors that best predict dropouts . . . are high absenteeism, being overage by two years, having low grades, and having a child. Using these factors should help identify a group of students with the highest probability of dropping out. Mark Dynarski and Philip Gleason found that these factors would in fact identify a group where one in three students would actually drop out. Although this rate is higher than the baseline 15 percent dropout rate that Dynarski and Gleason find based on the full sample of high school students, one could still question the use of these predictors to assign students to dropout-prevention programs. After all, a program serving students based on these predictors would serve many students who would not need the services and would fail to serve many students who would need them. Because most programs use a common set of risk factors to target students for intervention, Dynarski and Gleason's work helps to explain why so few programs show positive results, and it challenges program designers and practitioners to develop better ways to identify potential dropouts.

> "[Student] Dillan Hatcher said officials at Chestatee High School told him he was hurting the school's chances of meeting federal standards for its graduation rate."

Schools Lower Dropout Rates by Forcing Students to Go to Alternative Schools

Heather Vogell

Heather Vogell is an education reporter at the Atlanta Journal-Constitution. *In the following viewpoint, she reports that a number of students at the Hall County School District in Georgia were transferred to an alternative school, Lanier Career Academy, in the last weeks, or even week, of school. Vogell says that transferring students who fail the graduation tests can improve a school's statistics under the No Child Left Behind Act. Vogell suggests that Hall County schools may be trying to game the system to improve their numbers by transferring low-performing students.*

As you read, consider the following questions:

1. What did Hatcher say he did at Lanier after his transfer?

2. What did the *Atlanta Journal-Constitution* find about the number of transfers to Lanier from Hall County?

3. Why does Krysten Campbell believe transfers to Lanier have dropped at Hall County schools?

A Hall County student who transferred to an alternative school just days before graduation last year said this week [in May 2011] that the district all but forced him to go and provided none of the extra help administrators had promised.

Gaming the System

Dillan Hatcher said officials at Chestatee High School told him he was hurting the school's chances of meeting federal standards for its graduation rate. Hatcher failed one portion of the Georgia High School Graduation Test and, as a result, expected to receive a certificate of performance instead of a diploma. Only diplomas boost a school's graduation rate.

Hatcher said that when he arrived at Lanier Career Academy [LCA] the final week of school, educators told him it was too late in the year to enroll in any programs. He said he sat in front of a computer, texted friends and stared at the wall.

"I went for nothing," he said. "I should have just gone home."

Hall's practice of transferring struggling students from regular high schools to Lanier days before graduation has been criticized by some who questioned whether the district simply shuffled students around to game the state's accountability system. The pressure is much greater on regular high schools to meet graduation-rate standards than on Lanier.

Superintendent Will Schofield has vigorously defended the transfers. Last week, however, he said it is possible high schools had moved students to benefit their graduation rate in a few instances. But he said such transfers are not district practice.

"I would be pretty Pollyannaish if I said that that didn't happen at some point somewhere," he said. "But in terms of the whole philosophy of the program, that's not who we are."

At one point, West Hall High School was in the running for an award—a Blue Ribbon of Excellence—but missed adequate yearly progress, or AYP, by three students, he said. All the district had to do was transfer the three, he said, but school officials "took our lumps."

Overall, the district has defended sending students to Lanier, saying the moves are almost always voluntary and allow the district to provide assistance to students in danger of dropping out. Some are studying to retake the graduation test over the summer; others may take GED [general equivalency diploma] classes.

Enrollment in Lanier even at the end of the year improves chances students will continue in their studies, officials said.

Pressure to Move

The Hall district in northeast Georgia is only the latest school system to face accusations of monkeying with the numbers to try to improve schools' status under the accountability system built after the No Child Left Behind Act passed in 2001.

The *Atlanta Journal-Constitution* reported this month that, in the past three years, at least 94 Hall County students who were due to receive certificates instead of diplomas transferred to Lanier in the final days of the school year. A 2009 e-mail by the former principal for Lanier urged other schools to transfer their certificate students to Lanier at semester's end "to improve your graduation rate."

Since then, several students who were told by school officials to transfer to Lanier, or who knew students that did, talked with the newspaper about their experience.

The newspaper also performed additional data analysis that showed multiple years in which a small number of graduates made the difference between making and missing AYP for some Hall schools.

Hatcher said that, after he failed the graduation test, Chestatee High officials pulled him into the school office and told him he needed to go to Lanier. They convinced his father the move was good for him.

"They said you'll learn everything you need at LCA," said Hatcher, who was reluctant to leave the school he had attended since freshman year.

"When I got to LCA, they said, 'Get on the computer and do whatever,'" he said. "They said, 'It's too late in the year; we can't get you in a program.'"

He passed the graduation test re-test anyway. A few weeks later, he received his diploma.

"They threw me under the bus," said Hatcher, 18, who now works at his father's landscaping business.

Chestatee High principal Chip Underwood, who was assistant principal in 2010, said AYP typically isn't mentioned in such meetings. Last year, the school made AYP by a 21-diploma margin, data shows.

"I don't believe that to be the case at all," Underwood said of Hatcher's recollection he was told he would hurt the school's effort to meet federal standards. "We use LCA to help kids get graduated. Does it affect AYP? I think it does minutely."

Another former Chestatee student and friend of Hatcher's, Christian Beasley, said he, too, felt intense pressure from school officials to transfer the last week of school after he failed part of the graduation test.

"They transferred me before they even told me about it," he said. "They said they'd transferred my files to LCA and I had to start there on Monday."

School officials told him Lanier would help him pass the graduation test, he said. "They said it would be a good thing," he said.

Beasley's parents, however, objected. They didn't want him to receive his diploma from an alternative school, he said. He stayed at Chestatee and passed the graduation test anyway. "I don't know why they wanted to send me off," said Beasley, 19, who has a job doing maintenance, welding and fabricating.

Schofield said, given that Hall is a district of 26,000 students, a few may walk away not completely satisfied.

"Can you pick up a kid or two that is not happy with our experience? Absolutely," he said. "But there are an awful lot of positive stories."

Graduation Targets

Analysis of state data shows that for some Hall schools, every diploma mattered.

Three of Hall's traditional schools missed their graduation-rate targets in 2007. East Hall missed by 14 students. Chestatee was off by three students, state data shows. Johnson High missed by one.

Chestatee and Johnson still made AYP because of a second-chance option that allows schools that are close to the targets to use a multiyear average.

During the next two years, when transfers to Lanier soared district-wide, all three schools fared better.

East Hall made its graduation-rate goals by 10 students in 2008 and nine in 2009. Johnson succeeded as well, by 12 students in 2008 and 11 in 2009. Chestatee made the target by 18 students in 2008 and 14 in 2009.

During those two years, Hall high schools transferred a total of 79 students to Lanier at the last minute. State data obtained by the [*Atlanta Journal-Constitution*] does not show where the transfers originated.

Incentives for Administrators to Cheat

In the case of these standardized exams the pressure falls much more lightly on the students than on the teachers and administrators.... Since the exams don't affect the report cards they bring home, however, none of my children has ever shown much distress at a low exam score or elation at a high one.

The same cannot be said for the teachers and administrators over whose heads loom these annual state assessments necessitated by [the] No Child Left Behind [Act]. Buried within the provisions of the act, for example, are a series of steps which the government must take in response to a school that has underperformed on the exams and not responded to a set of initial corrective actions. Those steps include the following:

i) Reopening the school as a public charter school.

ii) Replacing all or most of the school staff (which may include the principal) who are relevant to the failure to make adequate yearly progress.

iii) Entering into a contract with an entity, such as a private management company, with a demonstrated record of effectiveness, to operate the public school.

Hence the state has been given power, as the second point indicates, in the case of schools where students are not performing effectively on the state exams, to fire all teachers and the principal.

James M. Lang, Cheating Lessons: Learning from Academic Dishonesty. *Cambridge, MA: Harvard University Press, 2013.*

Schofield said that, overall, the district has had great success in boosting graduates. Its graduation rate climbed by more than 11 percentage points, to about 79 percent, between 2007 and 2010. The Lanier transfers would not affect the district-wide rate.

For months, posters on local blogs have criticized Hall's late-semester transfers to Lanier.

Some traffic was generated by Krysten Campbell, a 22-year-old former Chestatee student who said several students have complained to her about being bullied to transfer to Lanier.

"It's just wrong what they're doing to these kids, especially their last week of their senior year," she said.

Campbell, a student at Gainesville State College, wrote Hall County School District officials to complain about the transfers as part of a class project. She then posted their responses on a local blog.

Hall officials have said that they expected few, if any, late transfers to Lanier this year. Campbell said she suspects that attention to the issue on blogs and in the media may be part of the reason.

"I guess that is kind of what it showed me: If I speak out loud enough, it can change," she said.

How We Got the Story

The *Atlanta Journal-Constitution* analyzed databases provided by the Georgia Department of Education for the 2008 through 2010 school years to determine when, and where, transfers were made in Hall County. The databases showed how many students earning certificates of performance transferred to Lanier Career Academy after May 1 each year. The state redacted the databases to remove potentially identifying information for small groupings of students, so it is possible that the actual number of transfers was slightly higher. The state also removed students' names to keep their records confidential. For this story, the [*Atlanta Journal-Constitution*] also analyzed a second state database that includes information on whether schools and districts met federal standards.

> "It can be a high-performing school be-
> cause they're kicking the students out."

At-Risk Students Are Forced into Alternative Schools

Scott Travis and Megan O'Matz

Scott Travis and Megan O'Matz are reporters for the Sun-
Sentinel, *the daily newspaper of Fort Lauderdale, Florida. In the
following viewpoint, they report that schools in Broward County,
Florida, are forcing some students into alternative programs.
Travis and O'Matz say that the school districts may be trying to
improve their graduation rates. They say that the alternative
programs are substandard and that the same programs were rejected in regular Broward County schools.*

As you read, consider the following questions:

1. According to the authors, what organization's standards
   does the Broward credit recovery program fail to meet?

2. How does Palm Beach County's dropout prevention
   program differ from Broward County's, according to the
   authors?

3. What is Apex Learning, according to the viewpoint?

Many of Broward County's struggling high school seniors have been called into their guidance counselors in recent weeks and strongly encouraged—some even say forced—to withdraw and finish their education through an online program.

Moved Out

The students are moved to one of eight off-campus learning centers at churches, community centers and shopping plazas where they do their work on computers and can come and go as they please.

They use a "credit recovery" program that fails to meet the standards for National Collegiate Athletic Association [NCAA] eligible athletes and one which the district discontinued in its regular high schools.

Some parents said they believe their schools are trying to shed low-performing students to boost their standing under the state's grading system, something the Broward school district strongly denies.

Dinorah Torres said her daughter, Erika, 17, was forced to withdraw from McArthur High School in Hollywood, a one-time D-rated school that now posts a sign in front of the school saying "Proud to Be an A School."

"It can be a high-performing school because they're kicking the students out," Torres said. "They gave me (an Oct. 25 deadline) to withdraw her and to bring her to the other school. So I was put up against a wall."

High schools are penalized under the state grading system if students drop out or fail to graduate in four years. But if those students transfer to an alternative school, they do not count as dropouts at the original school, even if they fail to get a diploma. Critics say schools usually wait to move students until after their official enrollment count in October, which is used to determine school funding.

Student Rachel Morga said McArthur "kicked out a lot of kids." Officials at McArthur declined comment, referring a call to the district's communications office.

Superintendent Robert Runcie said such allegations are untrue.

"We don't play those games. We just do what's in the best interest of the kids," he said. "If there's a program they need that may not be there, we may pursue other sites. Schools shouldn't be shifting kids. If we find out they are, we will address it, because we can't tolerate that."

Palm Beach County has a different approach to dropout prevention, using an online curriculum provider from another vendor at its regular high schools, said Eunice Greenfield, high school counseling specialist for that district.

The students "stay a part of our school," Greenfield said. "They go to school. They just go extra time. Like staying after school."

Broward County had 872 students enrolled at its off-campus learning centers. Classes are split into morning and afternoon sessions, from 7 a.m. to noon and from noon to 5 p.m.

But attendance is not compulsory. "Students can take the classes from home," Torres said she was told.

She said her daughter must be logged on for an hour to be counted as attending class.

The online programs allow students to focus on a deficient subject, rapidly progress through tests and prove they are competent in a subject faster than sitting in a classroom, district officials said. The traditional classroom isn't working for these students, said Marie Wright, director of instruction and intervention for Broward schools.

"They need a different model," she said.

Questionable Alternative Programs

Students at these schools take classes through Apex Learning, an online program used in more than 1,000 school systems around the country. But its implementation in Broward County has been problematic. Last year, the district received complaints that some high schools were administering Apex classes to student athletes without properly monitoring students, raising questions about potential cheating.

The NCAA determined that Broward's program failed its requirements and students could not use the courses to meet eligibility requirements. A football player at Morgan State University in Baltimore reported to Miramar High School that he had lost his NCAA scholarship because he made up an algebra class using the Apex program, according to an e-mail obtained by the *Sun-Sentinel*.

Apex, based in Seattle, offers an online program with its own teachers that is approved by the NCAA. But Broward's program uses its own staff to monitor it. Apex CEO [chief executive officer] Cheryl Vedoe said the company offers complete courses, but sometimes districts use only a portion of the course, a practice the NCAA doesn't allow.

Nick Sproull, assistant director of high school review for the NCAA, said the NCAA stopped allowing most fast-paced credit recovery programs around 2010.

"They're designed to be completed in a very short time, but the main problem is that they're designed to remove the role of instructor," he said. "We don't believe that is going to adequately prepare students for four-year universities."

Wright sent a letter to NCAA officials in August saying the Apex credit recovery was being dropped and would be replaced by the NCAA-approved Florida Virtual School for credit recovery.

But the online program is still being used at the off-campus learning centers.

Wright said the district doesn't have the funding to provide a full-staffed program at the off-campus sites or to use the Florida Virtual School. She also said the implementation is better at the alternative sites with "certified teachers interacting with students."

Still, whether the district continues the program is unclear. Runcie has directed principals and administrators to look at other options for struggling students in the future.

"We want to address any concerns out there and offer the widest array of opportunities to ensure students can stay current and on track with their credits," he said.

"Deaf schools are not just an educational option, but are the only beneficial placement for many deaf children."

Specialized Schools Are Vital for Hearing-Impaired Students

National Association of the Deaf

The National Association of the Deaf (NAD) is a nonprofit organization designed to empower deaf and hard of hearing individuals. In the following viewpoint, NAD argues that specialized schools for deaf students are vital for many deaf children and are in fact mandated in federal law. NAD adds that schools for deaf students are often the best place for children to learn American Sign Language. NAD concludes that schools for deaf students help children become productive adults, which benefits both the children and society as a whole.

As you read, consider the following questions:

1. What does NAD say is the most important benefit of specialized schools for deaf students?

2. What benefits does NAD say that schools for deaf students provide for other schools in the district?

3. According to NAD, what do states need to do in terms of transportation for schools for deaf students?

The National Association of the Deaf (NAD) recognizes the value of schools for the deaf and cherishes their contributions to the education and development of deaf and hard of hearing children for nearly 200 years. Deaf schools are critical to the education of deaf and hard of hearing (hereinafter "deaf") children, and every effort must be made to preserve them. NAD strongly supports the continuation and strengthening of these schools.

Schools for Deaf Students Are a Necessity

Deaf schools are not just an educational option, but are the only beneficial placement for many deaf children. The Individuals with Disabilities Education Act requires that states provide a "continuum of alternative placements," which includes "instruction in regular classes, special classes, *special schools*, home instruction, and hospitals and institutions." (34 C.F.R. § 300.115) (Emphasis added.) Schools for the deaf are not optional, but are a mandated placement under law.

Schools for the deaf have been considered during state budget cuts, but often the costs are significantly higher to provide educational services in other settings. Placing deaf children in their respective neighborhood schools with the provision of communication access services can be extremely costly and, in some locations, simply not feasible due to limited human resources. There are barely enough qualified teachers of the deaf and qualified educational interpreters to meet current needs, and not nearly enough of such professionals to serve every neighborhood school that has a deaf child residing in the district. Placing every deaf child in their respective neighborhood school is not practical, economical, nor educationally beneficial. In many states, there are large geographical areas with a small deaf student population, making schools for the deaf a cost-effective means to optimal educational services.

Deaf schools, an integral part of American history, have not only received quality education but also benefited from the fostering of its culture, heritage, and language through such essential institutions. Schools for the deaf, including charter schools founded to serve deaf children, are uniquely capable of providing the necessary visual learning environment and the ideal conditions for language development for deaf children.

Most importantly, deaf children can only begin to learn when they acquire language, which is a human and linguistic right, and this acquisition is optimally achieved in American Sign Language (ASL). ASL provides a solid language base, through which deaf children can further develop their cognitive and academic education to grow into contributing, successful adults. The value of teachers communicating directly with their students cannot be emphasized enough; educating children indirectly through interpreters or technologies is not effective or efficient, especially with respect to the initial steps of language acquisition.

No other educational setting can offer the spontaneity and freedom of communication found in schools for the deaf. Schools for the deaf are unique and provide a community of genuine membership for many deaf children. Students in these schools develop emotional, social and cognitive abilities that are crucial to realizing human potential and identity. They provide extracurricular activities, leadership opportunities, and mentoring by successful deaf and hard of hearing adult role and language models. Students are part of a critical mass of age-appropriate peers and common-language users and experience authentic peer interaction. Schools for the deaf provide students with an inclusive, high-quality education with high expectations, highly qualified teachers, and a rigorous general education curriculum.

Schools for the deaf also serve as statewide resource centers for all school districts to utilize when needed. They offer a wealth of expertise on all aspects of educating deaf children. Such centers provide valuable tools for information and referrals, technical assistance, professional development training, curriculum design, and media and materials exchange. They are also primary resources on ASL. Some schools for the deaf offer specialized services to support deaf students placed in their neighborhood schools. All school districts are encouraged to tap into the expertise of the professionals at schools for the deaf.

Without deaf schools, educating deaf children becomes more costly both in the short term with limitations in human and other resources and in the long term with educational deficiencies.

The choice is clear: with schools for the deaf, society benefits with more productive and contributing deaf adults. Schools for the deaf have produced thousands of productive members of our society and are critical for the continued development of deaf community leadership in our nation.

Call to Action

State support of schools. States must provide strong support to their school(s) for the deaf. This includes providing adequate funding, facilities, referrals, and other resources to the schools, and support to university programs to provide a source of teachers and other trained personnel.

Language-driven placements. Decisions about educational placements for deaf children should be guided by considerations of language. That is, deaf children should be placed in an educational setting that supports their language and communication access and development. The "least restrictive environment" for a deaf child is a "language rich environment"— and for many of these children it is a specialized setting, not necessarily the regular education environment.

Parent choice. Parents must have a protected right to choose a school for the deaf for their child's placement. For this pa-

Saved by Schools for the Deaf

There are those who believe they were "rescued" by schools for the deaf, and their memories are of leaving behind unbearably lonely homes for an environment of friends and adults who could sign and communicate with them. One eighty-year-old deaf man we interviewed lost his mother when he was five and was sent to live with his hearing aunt on a family farm during the Depression. He hated the summers of grinding labor, but worse, he could hardly bear the oppressive solitude among his hearing relatives. His deaf father rarely visited, leaving him entirely in the care of relatives who were exhausted from hard farm labor and had little left to give him. From 1928 to 1940, when he left for Gallaudet [a school for deaf students in Washington, DC], he lived at his school from September to June, and returned to his aunt's farm only during Christmas and in the summers, even though the farm was but a thirty-minute drive from the school. For him, the school became a respite and the closest semblance of family that he could imagine. . . .

Even in the modern context, schools for the deaf continue to "rescue" children, particularly adolescents who struggle to succeed in public schools. Even at a time when distances are short, and information is easy and readily available, isolation still happens. Instead of being caused by geographical remoteness or family income, isolation can be caused by neglect, indifference, or simply lack of expectation. It is not uncommon to find ten- or eleven-year-old deaf children who arrive at schools for the deaf barely literate, knowing not even how to spell or write their last names.

Carol Padden and Tom Humphries, Inside Deaf Culture. *Cambridge, MA: Harvard University Press, 2005, pp. 14–15.*

rental right to remain protected, states must ensure continued funding of schools for the deaf. States should ensure that parents and local school districts support the choice of a school for the deaf as a viable placement option.

Collaboration. States should develop and facilitate collaborations between the school(s) for the deaf and the statewide communities of deaf people, parents, professionals and local school districts. For the optimal benefit of deaf children, states should form some sort of committee or task force comprising representation from these statewide communities. Through such groups, the entities can work together on issues that will improve education for deaf and hard of hearing children in the state.

Accountability. Schools for the deaf must be included in state accountability systems in ways that are meaningful and support improvements in outcomes for deaf and hard of hearing students. Schools for the deaf should follow and be accountable for the public education curriculum in their state or locality.

Personnel preparation. States must have meaningful standards for personnel preparation, curriculum, and access by the students to all staff and programs. Staff should be ASL fluent, culturally competent, and highly qualified in core academic subjects.

Transportation. States should support safe and adequate transportation, including transportation for extracurricular activities, for children to schools for the deaf. States should clarify which agency is responsible for providing transportation. Without the means to attend the school, the child's right to attend the school is compromised.

| "Clearly, these students did not appear to have social skill difficulties greater than one might find in the general population."

Hearing-Impaired Students Do Well Socially in Mainstream Classrooms

Shirin D. Antia, Patricia Jones, John Luckner, Kathryn H. Kreimeyer, and Susanne Reed

Shirin D. Antia is a professor of special education at the University of Pittsburgh; Patricia Jones is a statistical consultant at the University of Arizona; John Luckner is a professor of special education at the University of Northern Colorado; Kathryn H. Kreimeyer is an adjunct associate professor in the Department of Disability and Psychoeducational Studies at the University of Arizona; and Susanne Reed is a researcher at the University of Arizona. In the following viewpoint, the authors report on a study of the social skills of deaf and hard of hearing (DHH) students in general education classrooms. They find that DHH stu-

Shirin D. Antia, Patricia Jones, John Luckner, Kathryn H. Kreimeyer, and Susanne Reed, "Social Outcomes of Students Who Are Deaf and Hard of Hearing in General Education Classrooms," *Exceptional Children*, vol. 77, no. 4, 2011, pp. 489–504. Copyright © 2011 by Council for Exceptional Children. All rights reserved. Reproduced by permission.

dents have social skills similar to their non-hearing-impaired peers. They conclude that DHH students succeed well in general education classrooms.

As you read, consider the following questions:

1. Why do the authors argue that social relationships are important?

2. On what research questions did the authors focus?

3. What are some of the reasons the authors give for the difference in results between their study and previous research?

Students with hearing loss attending general education class-rooms have been reported to experience difficulties in social skills and relationships. This 5-year longitudinal study examined the social skills and problem behaviors of students who were deaf or hard of hearing, and who attended general education class-rooms. Data were obtained from classroom teachers and students themselves. The mean social skills and problem behavior scores were within the average range and normally distributed each year. The average change over 5 years in social skills and problem behavior was not significant. The most consistent predictors of social outcomes were the students' classroom communication participation and participation in extracurricular activities. Implications for placement, intervention, and further research are discussed.

The Importance of Social Relationships

Social relationships add quality to one's life and contribute to one's ability to think and learn. A growing body of research indicates that having good social skills is critical for succeeding in society, including success in the labor market. Research also documents the negative impact of a lack of social skills. [L.K.] Elksnin and [N.] Elksnin indicated that individuals who lack social skills are often rejected by others and are at risk for developing mental health problems that persist during adulthood. [M.] Bullis, [V.] Nishioka, [H.D.B.] Fredericks, and [C.] Davis reported that 90% of job loss is related to social skills problems rather than an inability to do the job.

Children and youth with hearing loss (also described as *deaf or hard of hearing*; DHH) often have communication difficulties and consequently may not develop appropriate social skills and social relationships. [K.] Meadow suggested that communication and language difficulties resulted in experiential deficiencies that negatively influenced social development. Researchers and practitioners have been particularly concerned about the social outcomes of students with hearing loss who attend public school programs where their classmates are primarily hearing, because of problems with peer communication and interaction.

Social Outcomes of DHH Children and Adolescents

Social outcomes can be examined through several lenses including social interactions with hearing peers, peer relationships and friendships, and ratings of social skills and behavior.

Social Interaction

Observation research on the peer interactions of elementary students who are DHH indicates that those who spend limited time in general education classes engage in infrequent interaction with hearing classmates. However, adolescent self-reports of peer interactions are contradictory. English adolescents reported that they interacted equally or more frequently with hearing peers than with peers who were DHH, whereas U.S. and Canadian adolescents reported the opposite.

Peer Relationships

Students who are DHH in general education settings may have poorer social relationships than hearing students. Researchers have reported significantly lower likeability, social preference, and acceptance ratings for elementary students who are DHH when compared to hearing peers; these low ratings did not change over time, despite opportunities for peer social interaction. [T.] Nunes and [U.] Pretzlik found that elementary students were as likely as their hearing peers to be popular or rejected, but were significantly less likely to have friends in their class. In contrast, [L.] Wauters and [H.] Knoors found no difference in social status between elementary Dutch students with or without hearing loss over a 2-year period. Adolescents with hearing loss in general education settings have reported higher emotional security with peers who were DHH than with peers who were not.

Social Skills

Social skills are usually measured through rating scales and interviews. [E.O.] Andersson, [A.] Rydell, and [H.C.] Larsen compared the social competence and behavioral problems of elementary-age Swedish students with hearing loss enrolled in general education programs and similar-age students without hearing loss. Neither parents nor teachers reported differences between the two groups in prosocial orientation, social competence, or externalizing and internalizing problems. [L.] Mejstad, [K.] Heiling, and [C.G.] Svedin found similar positive results with Swedish students. [B.A.] Kent used a student self-report measure to compare the psychosocial behaviors of New Zealand adolescents with and without hearing loss, and reported no differences in loneliness or sense of belonging at school.

Factors Influencing Social Outcomes

Although multiple factors contribute to social outcomes, the most studied is the mode of communication and communication skill of students with hearing loss. [J.] Dammeyer reported that poor sign or spoken communication skills were significantly related to psychosocial difficulties. [M.S.] Stinson and [K.] Whitmire found that adolescents with hearing loss who preferred to use oral communication reported more frequent social participation with hearing peers, and [C.] Musselman, [A.] Mootilal, and [S.] MacKay found that oral English competence contributed to feelings of security and interaction with hearing peers.

The effect of degree of hearing loss on social outcomes is of considerable interest. Although it is expected that children with a greater degree of hearing loss will have poorer social outcomes, research indicates that children with all degrees of hearing loss have social difficulties. In some studies, students with mild and moderate hearing losses have scored below hearing norms on various aspects of social behavior—although other studies have found no significant differences. Although children with mild hearing loss may have poorer social outcomes than their hearing peers, it is not clear that children with a greater degree of hearing loss have more severe social problems than those with lesser degree of hearing loss. Neither [J.M.] Davis et al., [K.] Furstenberg and [G.] Doyal, nor Dammeyer found a relationship between students' social functioning and degree of hearing loss. However, Furstenberg et al. reported a positive relationship between good social outcomes and students' use of their hearing as measured by knowledge of their own hearing loss and listening devices, and use of residual hearing. [T.] Most reported that, although teacher-rated social behavior of Arab-Israeli children was related to degree of hearing loss, those with severe loss received better ratings than those with minimal loss.

Familiarity with peers can impact social outcomes, specifically the quality of peer interaction. [S.D.] Antia, [K.H.] Kreimeyer, and [N.] Eldredge reported that interaction increased among students with and without hearing loss when they participated in activities that promoted familiarity. Stinson and Whitmire found that English adolescents with hearing loss reported higher emotional security with hearing peers as they spent more time in general education classrooms, although the opposite was true of American adolescents (Stinson et al., 1996). Similarly, [D.A] Stewart and Stinson reported that adolescents with hearing loss who were involved in structured school social activities were more likely to make friends and to participate in social activities with hearing peers. Frequency of participation in these activities was associated with high levels of social competence.

Finally, family involvement in children's social lives can influence social outcomes. Parents serve as social "coaches" for their children by discussing strategies for making friends or for handling peer problems and by demonstrating competent social interaction with a variety of individuals. Parental resources may affect social outcomes: Families with money or time can provide access to extracurricular activities that provide opportunities for socializing with peers.

Purpose of the Current Study

Our review of the social outcomes literature for students with hearing loss indicates that although several studies show positive outcomes, especially for elementary students, studies of adolescent students show mixed outcomes. It is not clear whether students' social outcomes become more negative as they get older, or whether the differences are due to varying characteristics of the samples and school contexts. Further, much of the previous research was undertaken with students who spent only a small part of their school day with hearing peers. In contrast, an estimated 52% of students with hearing loss currently spend more than 80% of their school day in general education classrooms with hearing peers. In many cases, these students are the only ones with hearing loss in the classroom or even in the school. Because these students are difficult to find, little information is available on their social outcomes.

The purpose of this study was to examine the social outcomes of U.S. students with hearing loss attending general education classrooms for 2 or more hours per day. In order to determine whether changes occurred over time, we obtained data on students annually over a 5-year period. The specific research questions were:

1. How do general education teachers rate the social skills of students with hearing loss in their classrooms and how do these ratings change over time?

2. How do students with hearing loss in general education classrooms rate their own social skills and how do these ratings change over time?

3. Are there differences in teacher and student ratings of social skills?

4. What factors influence social skills? . . .

DHH Students Do Well in General Classrooms

A large body of evidence indicates that the possession of adequate social skills is necessary for maintaining social, psychological, and occupational well-being. Although general education placements may be beneficial in terms of academic outcomes, the social experiences of students in these placements are perceived as less positive than in separate classes or schools. Therefore, the most important finding in this study is that, for this sample of students, the mean social skill ratings given by teachers, and the self-ratings of students themselves, are similar to those reported for the normative sample. Clearly, these students did not appear to have social skill difficulties greater than one might find in the general population. In addition, our data show that these positive social outcomes remained stable over 5 years.

There are several reasons for the differences in results between this study and previous research. Most of the students in this sample spent the majority of their day in general education classes whereas previous studies included mostly students who were in general education classes for a limited time. Thus, these students were more likely than those in previous studies to be familiar with their peers and to be members of—not visitors to—the classroom. Also, most students were in their neighborhood schools, and thus had a chance to know their peers both in and out of the classroom. Many of the students in this sample, in contrast to students studied by other researchers, were hard of hearing rather than deaf and used oral language to communicate, minimizing communication difficulties between them and their hearing peers.

The incidence of problem behaviors as reported by teachers was similar to that of the norming sample of the SSRS [social skills rating system]. Although some researchers have reported a high incidence of social-emotional problems in students with hearing loss, these studies typically included only those in self-contained settings with a (possibly) high percentage of students with additional disabilities. Researchers who have studied students who are DHH in general education settings outside of the United States have not reported high rates of problem behaviors.

An important finding is that most students did not show a decrease in social skills nor an increase in behavior problems over time. Concerns have been expressed regarding the social outcomes of adolescents who have hearing loss and who have little contact with peers similar to themselves. Although we do not have data regarding the amount of contact that students had with peers with hearing loss outside of the school setting, it seems clear that the presence of primarily hearing peers in school did not negatively impact social outcomes.

It could be argued that general education teachers provide a somewhat rosy picture of the skills of students with hearing loss. The advantage of asking general education teachers to rate the students is that their reference group is likely to be students who are hearing—unlike the reference group for teachers of DHH students, who are likely to be other students with hearing loss. Our local reliability data and the normally distributed teacher ratings indicate that the teachers did not provide overly positive ratings of students. Moreover, student self-ratings were also normally distributed.

Social skills ratings are only one way to examine social outcomes. Although students may rate themselves high on social skills, they may lack close friends or satisfying social relationships. Thus, further research with different samples of students and different dependent variables is warranted. However, it is important to examine the issues faced by the approximately 25% of students who showed decreases in social skills. These students may need specific and ongoing interventions to improve their social outcomes.

Variables Influencing Social Outcomes

It is important to note that almost all the variables we selected had some relationship with social skills and problem behavior scores, with the exception of degree of hearing loss and frequency of teacher-parent communication. Our findings are consistent with those of some other researchers regarding the effects of degree of hearing loss on both social and academic outcomes. This is not to argue that hearing loss does not affect outcomes. However, degree of hearing loss is often used as a proxy variable for communication abilities. With the advent of new technology (i.e., cochlear implants and digital hearing aids), effective early intervention, and appropriate support in general education classrooms, degree of hearing loss may not be a good predictor of outcomes, and perhaps should not be used as a major indicator when decisions are made regarding educational placement. In contrast, functional hearing, which is a measure of the students' ability to use residual hearing (with amplification) within the classroom setting, appeared to influence teacher ratings of social skills. Although functional hearing might be related to degree of hearing loss, it is also related to appropriate use of amplification and the acoustic environment in which students function.

Classroom communication participation was a consistent predictor of social outcomes. Appropriate classroom participation can influence the attitudes of peers and teachers towards the student, and positively affect relationships inside and outside the classroom. Participation in school and community activities was another consistent predictor of social outcomes. Although professionals have suggested that participation in extracurricular activities can contribute to the social well-being of students who are DHH, this study is the first to provide empirical support.

Implications and Limitations

Professionals may need to revise their assumptions that students with hearing loss attending general education classrooms are likely to have negative social outcomes. At the same time, because social skills and problem behaviors seem to be stable over time, professionals should not assume that students who exhibit poor social skills or frequent problem behaviors will change without intervention. If students with hearing loss are to be well integrated socially, they need to have opportunities to positively interact with peers. Indeed, such positive interaction has been a reason to argue that students with significant hearing loss should attend center-based programs. Data from this study support attempts by parents to include their children in extracurricular and community activities. Parents and teachers may need to advocate for interpreters and transportation to allow students with hearing loss to be included in school extracurricular activities.

Classroom participation is influenced by students' communication skills and the environment. Physical aspects of the classroom, notably classroom noise, can be abated by changing the classroom physical configuration and noise-reducing modifications. Teachers of students who are DHH should consider it part of their professional role to work with classroom teachers and school administrators to improve classroom communication conditions.

As with any single piece of research, there are several limitations to this study. The students were selected from only two states. In addition, our research would have been enhanced by obtaining social skill ratings from teachers of DHH students and parents.

In order to obtain buy-in from school districts and teachers, we selected measures that were teacher- and student-friendly and took a short amount of time to administer. Some of these measures (e.g., the functional ratings and the parental participation measure) may not be sensitive to small differences among students. More sensitive measures might have resulted in a different set of predictors for social outcomes. Finally, even though our analyses pointed to particular variables that influence social outcomes, it is important to note that the amount of variability explained is modest. Clearly there are other variables that were not measured, or perhaps not measured with sufficiently sensitive instruments, that influence social outcomes.

Children with hearing loss are increasingly likely to attend general education classrooms for several reasons including early identification, early intervention, and better access to auditory information. These factors are likely to result in better language and communication outcomes, which, in turn, will result in local, rather than special school placements. Although results of some previous research pointed to negative social outcomes for students in general education settings, this study indicates that social outcomes may, on the contrary, be quite positive. Thus parents and professionals may not have to opt for positive academic outcomes at the cost of positive social outcomes. Good classroom communication participation and participation in extracurricular activities, areas in which inter-vention is possible, appear to positively influence social out-comes.

| "Is the child breathing? Then they belong in a regular class."

Children with Mental Disabilities Should Be Included in Mainstream Classrooms

Nirvi Shah

Nirvi Shah is a writer and the education editor at Politico Pro. In the following viewpoint, she argues that students with mental disabilities benefit from inclusion in regular classes. Students in special education classes are often isolated and do not learn necessary real-life skills. When they are included in regular class, Shah argues, the students thrive and make friends. Shah concludes that school districts need to make provisions to include all students in regular classrooms.

As you read, consider the following questions:

1. According to Shah, why aren't children with disabilities mainstreamed despite the clarity of the law?

2. Why does Ricki Sabia say that her son should read Shakespeare?

3. What social norms are often not enforced in special education classrooms, according to Sue Davis-Killian?

It has been more than 30 years since the federal government first declared that children with different abilities shouldn't be automatically separated from one another in school. Julia Horsman's parents, and others all over the country, are still fighting to have the law enforced. Too often, they say, school administrators' first instincts are separation, not inclusion.

Change Is Needed Now

"But when you read the law it's so clear-cut," says Julia's mother, Lisa Horsman.

The problem is that the radical changes the law promised never sunk in at the ground level—namely, in teacher-education programs, says Kathleen Whitbread, an associate professor of education at [the University of] Saint Joseph in Connecticut.

The latest figures from the U.S. Department of Education show that, overall, almost 57 percent of students with disabilities spend the majority of their day in traditional classrooms. But that number masks a wide range of outcomes for a diverse group of students. For students with mental retardation, for example, the inclusion rate is less than 16 percent.

"Change is slow, yes," Whitbread says, "but this is ridiculous."

When Whitbread was studying to be a teacher in the early 1980s, her special education classes didn't include teachers learning to be math or kindergarten or chemistry teachers.

"All of the students in my classes were special-ed teachers," she said. "We were focusing on things like behavioral modification, functional skills, teaching kids how to tie their shoes and brush their teeth." Then she met an inclusion activist who put things in perspective for her.

"She said, 'Is the child breathing? Then they belong in a regular class,'" Whitbread says. "I think that people respond to the civil rights argument, that it's wrong to separate children. Would you put all the blue-eyed children in one classroom? Of course you wouldn't."

While Saint Joseph and a small number of teacher-training programs no longer have separate tracks for special education teachers and everyone else, Whitbread says the combined approach remains uncommon.

She and other advocates say the time has passed—though not everyone has accepted it—for special education to be thought of as a place, instead of a service.

"Teaching is about taking the child that you get and using what you've learned to reach this child," Whitbread says. "This is what we should have been doing in 1976."

The Case for Inclusion

Early on, Julia was in a separate classroom but the teacher seemed passionate and her daughter seemed to be learning, Lisa Horsman recalled. Isolated, but educated.

Then the teachers seemed to stop caring.

And Julia stopped learning.

"I went in there to watch one day and the teacher said 'Let's go back to the reading we were reading yesterday,'" Horsman said. "They had nothing to look at, nothing to follow. They were seven or eight little zombies sitting there, with their desks cleared off."

After watching Julia languish in that separate room—where all the other students were boys—she decided she couldn't let the school district in Prince George's County, Maryland, make decisions for her anymore.

"I [had done] what I thought was best for my kid, what the doctors told me, what the school told me," she says. "And I was punished for it."

Horsman called the Maryland Coalition for Inclusive Education, where attorney Selene Almazan took on Julia's case.

"I represent families who want their children to go to their neighborhood school," Almazan says. "Really, it's just an enforcement of what their child is legally entitled to."

"There's been some progress," she says, but "it is not uniform across the country. There is this whole idea that with kids with disabilities, you need to take care of them. It really is rather paternalistic in many ways, rather than looking at each individual child. I'm hard-pressed to find where there's good education in these segregated classrooms."

It's no wonder, she says, that many schools continue to assume these same children won't be successful in a regular classroom, she says.

"I've found that the opposite is true," she says.

As with Julia.

And an experience like Julia's is possible only if schools put in the effort to make inclusion meaningful.

"As kids started to spend more time in regular classes, then we had to fight for teaching them," Whitbread says. "That to me has been the more frustrating fight."

"Who Wrote Holden Caulfield?"

For many parents of children with disabilities who manage to get their children included, their work is far from over. Many say they have turned into part-time teachers once their kids make it into a regular classroom.

Ricki Sabia says creating study guides and finding supplemental materials for her son has been a part of her life for years—on top of her work as a lawyer and on the staff of the National Down Syndrome Society.

Her son, Steve, is in the 11th grade and has Down syndrome. When the rest of his class read the *Odyssey*, Steve read the 130-page abridged version, watched the movie and used a computer program that tested his comprehension.

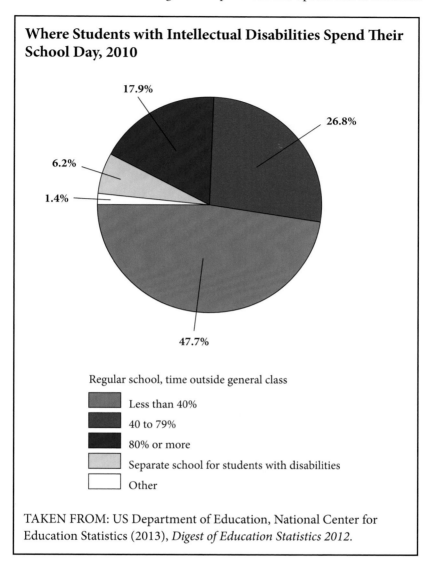

Where Students with Intellectual Disabilities Spend Their School Day, 2010

17.9%

26.8%

6.2%

1.4%

47.7%

Regular school, time outside general class

Less than 40%

40 to 79%

80% or more

Separate school for students with disabilities

Other

TAKEN FROM: US Department of Education, National Center for Education Statistics (2013), *Digest of Education Statistics 2012.*

When his class read Shakespeare, she found something called "No Fear Shakespeare," which had the original text on one side of the page and its modern English translation on the other.

"Why should he read Shakespeare? Why is that important for any kid?" Sabia says. "To broaden his horizons. To have common experiences. To see what he likes and to shape what he is going to do. When he's on the subway and he sees a picture of Shakespeare, he knows who that is."

Getting through *The Catcher in the Rye* was particularly difficult, she says, because she couldn't find this novel—centered on one character's feelings of alienation—in any other format. Still, her son plodded through it. And the experience stuck with Steve, a boy the Maryland school system wanted to teach how to sweep floors, run a washing machine and cook.

"He likes the band Green Day, and they have this song, 'Who Wrote Holden Caulfield?'" she says. "He knew what that was."

Sabia says the development of curricula designed for all kinds of learners is finally happening on a large scale, such as Universal Design for Learning, created by the Center for Applied Special Technology in Massachusetts. It offers a blueprint for teachers working with students with varying needs. . . .

Even without an investment in a ready-made curriculum like Universal Design, the inclusion process might go more smoothly if all teachers in a school were to collaborate, Whitbread says.

Well-trained special education teachers already know many unique ways to reach children who have different learning styles, Whitbread says. If one approach doesn't work, they will know of another.

But if individual classroom teachers continue to be confronted with reinventing these approaches each time they have a student with disabilities, inclusion can seem impossible.

"It's always been 'Special education? You go there,'" says Sharon Leonard, an educational consultant at the Pennsylvania Training and Technical Assistance Network. Instead, Leonard says, teachers should see special education as a service they bring to the student. "We can't get a better placement than that general education classroom."

Learning the Ways of the World

For Julia Horsman, life at her old school, in that separate classroom, was lonely. As the only girl, she was already isolated. She learned some vulgar words from the boys in her class, which she repeated at home. Her sweet temperament turned sullen.

She stopped smiling, says her mother.

But school district administrators warned that Julia would be just as isolated in a regular class. They said she would fail. They said she would be miserable.

The Horsmans consulted a neuropsychologist, who had a different vision. He expected Julia to blossom, and predicted that other kids would be nurturing.

"It was exactly the way the neuropsychologist said," Lisa Horsman says. "The teacher said, 'Whenever I would tell the kids to pair up, everybody would be fighting over Julia.'"

Almazan, who helped get Julia into her inclusive setting, notes that Julia didn't just raise her reading level during her first year in a regular classroom.

"She got birthday party invitations," Almazan says. "When a child is a part of the classroom and accepted by peers, peers get it. Kids know when another child needs help. Kids are the ones that can tell another kid, 'You're not supposed to hit.'"

Sue Davis-Killian's daughter Lisa has Down syndrome, and Davis-Killian insisted on full-time inclusion in Florida schools. Beyond her firm belief that Lisa will get a real education in an inclusive setting, Davis-Killian wants her daughter to learn the ways of the real world.

"Most adults with cognitive disabilities are unemployed," Davis-Killian notes. "And the biggest reason that they lose their jobs is that they don't understand the rules: They don't show up on time or don't show up at all. They don't listen to the boss."

In segregated classes, Davis-Killian says, too often there is no reinforcement of basic social norms, like being on time.

Special education buses often arrive at school late and leave early, she says. But for Lisa, an eighth grader, school starts at 9 a.m., period.

"She knows she can't just go walking into class whenever she wants," Davis-Killian says.

Behaviors that can draw attention to a particular disability aren't curbed in segregated classrooms, she says.

Like many people with cognitive disabilities, Lisa had her own soothing behavior. Lisa would put her head down and make a humming noise.

"It took me and the school two years of saying, 'Get your head up' to stop her from doing that," she says. "I saw another girl in a segregated classroom and watched for 15 minutes as she hummed to herself. She was 6. Nobody ever said anything."

The teachers in the special-ed classroom "don't hear it anymore," Davis-Killian says, while in a regular classroom, it wouldn't be tolerated. "That behavior will incredibly limit what you can do in life," she says.

From her life of inclusion, Lisa has learned hip lingo, and she knows how to send text messages to her friends—and how to delete the call logs so her mother doesn't know she made calls after bedtime.

"It's not that she doesn't do anything different—she does have Down syndrome," her mother says. "But that's the aspect that inclusion can't quantify: She still doesn't realize that she's different."

Included

After all the years of fighting over Julia Horsman's placement in her neighborhood school, her inclusive status will become uncertain again when she heads to middle school next fall.

The school district only agreed to a two-year trial, at the end of which they will evaluate Julia to see whether she should go back to a segregated setting.

Tina Progar's son Patrick was included from kindergarten through middle school. But when Patrick, who has Down syndrome, entered high school two years ago, the district balked. They say they don't have the resources to make general education classes fit Patrick's needs. So now he spends most of his day in a special education classroom with other teenagers who have a variety of disabilities.

"Pat's life is now part of a group," says Progar, of Maryland. "He is now a special-ed kid."

Her once-independent son with a knack for technology, a host of friends and a sharp sense of humor has become withdrawn.

And Progar is exhausted. As she continues to plead with the school to let Patrick spend more time in general education classes, she is working on another project. She wants to find a place for Patrick to spend part of his day volunteering, which would give him the opportunity to socialize and regain some of his independence.

"I have gone before the school board. I joined a group that's working for the least restrictive environment for kids with disabilities," she says. "All of these families are getting burned out. And I cannot wait for my son to get out of school.

"Inclusion can be law in the books, but this is an attitude issue."

For now, Julia Horsman is just one of the kids at her school. Julia still takes time out of class for occupational therapy, so she can master things like opening zippers, but otherwise, her mom says, "I almost forget she's in special ed. There's so much less fighting to do."

At a parent-teacher organization meeting last school year, Lisa Horsman ran into Julia's principal, Justin FitzGerald.

"I know there was some reluctance to have her," Horsman told him, but "she's where she belongs."

He looked at her and replied: "Absolutely."

> *"They are celebrated at special educa-*
> *tion centers for their abilities, not their*
> *inabilities."*

Inclusion Does Not Benefit Disabled Students

Barbara Jones

Barbara Jones is a staff writer for the Los Angeles Daily News. *In the following viewpoint, she reports that parents of special education students in the Los Angeles Unified School District are protesting the decision to move their children from specialized schools to general education classrooms. The parents believe that the special education centers provide their children with a nurturing environment and that their children will be ostracized and less well served in a mainstream classroom. Jones reports that the parents say the decision to mainstream children should be their choice, not the school district's.*

As you read, consider the following questions:

1. According to Jones, how many schools and students will be affected by the changes in the Los Angeles Unified School District?

2. Why did protesters target the office of Tamar Galatzan?

3. Who will be affected by the merger of the Frances Blend school with Van Ness elementary, according to the viewpoint?

Waving signs and chanting "Our kids, our choice," scores of Los Angeles Unified [School District, LAUSD] parents and teachers protested the looming transfer of hundreds of disabled students from special education centers to traditional schools, as the district complies with laws to integrate students who have physical and developmental challenges.

Parents Want to Choose

The protesters oppose the merger of four special education centers with nearby traditional schools, a move that will affect about 300 disabled youngsters when school starts next month [August 2013]. Opponents of the plan say the district will be segregating rather than integrating their kids by putting them in unsafe situations and setting them up for teasing or bullying. They say they want it to be their choice, not the district's, to transfer their kids to a traditional campus.

"They are celebrated at special education centers for their abilities, not their inabilities," said Rhonda Berrios of West Hills, whose 19-year-old son, Michael, is profoundly autistic. "They have dances, and basketball and baseball teams and cheerleading squads. . . . The district wants to throw them into a one-size-fits-all environment, and that would be a travesty if this happens."

Michael is now enrolled at [Diane S.] Leichman special education center in Reseda, which under the district's plan will begin shifting high school students to traditional campuses in 2014. Berrios and others demonstrated for about 90 minutes in the sweltering heat on behalf of their children and those who might lose what they see as the advantages of a protected environment.

Tom Williamson of North Hills said his son Blair, who has Down syndrome, learned self-confidence and life skills during the years he spent at Leichman. Blair, now a 34-year-old actor, has credits that include roles on *CSI* and *Scrubs*.

"He learned to go from classroom to classroom, and to the cafeteria," Williamson said.

"He was given freedom and independence that he wouldn't have had at a general education campus."

The 100 or so demonstrators targeted the office of school board member Tamar Galatzan, saying four of the district's 14 special-ed centers are located in her west San Fernando Valley district. Her office is also next door to the shuttered West Valley Special Education Center, a building that now houses Daniel Pearl [Magnet] High [School]. Protesters complained that Galatzan did nothing to block the closure of West Valley, although that was never a board decision.

Galatzan was working at her full-time job as a city prosecutor on Wednesday and was not at her LAUSD office, a spokeswoman said. Questions were referred to Sharyn Howell, executive director of LAUSD's Special Education Division, which serves about 83,000 students. Howell noted that the district is bound by federal and state law, as well as a federal consent decree, to mainstream more special education students and give handicapped youngsters more opportunities to interact with kids at traditional campuses. "We're talking about physical education, arts types of programs, computer labs and library time," she said. "This is a chance to get the students with their siblings, cousins and neighborhood kids at a general education site."

They will continue to have classroom lessons that are appropriate for their level of learning, along with the aides, nurses, therapists and other supports they've had in the past, she added.

Shifting Students

Los Angeles Unified spends nearly $1.5 billion annually on special education programs, which have shifted over the years from stand-alone centers to mainstream classrooms. Beginning last year, preschoolers who might previously have been enrolled in special-ed centers started their education at a traditional school. Several demonstrators say they believe district officials are trying to whittle down the enrollment so they can eventually close all of the centers—a move that Howell has previously denied. The district currently operates 14 special-ed centers, which last year served 2,190 students.

Under the plan set to take effect in August, [Joaquin] Miller special-ed center in Reseda will transfer about 100 students to Cleveland [Charter] High [School] but will continue to provide its career-training program for ages 18–22.

About two dozen youngsters from Lull Special Education Center in Encino will enroll in Reseda High, the first step in transforming the facility to one for elementary students only. Next year, middle schoolers will go to [James] Madison [Middle School]. Fifty kids at [James J.] McBride school in Venice will go to Grand View elementary, and [Benjamin] Banneker [Charter Public] School, near downtown L.A., will send 60 youngsters to Avalon Gardens [Elementary School]. The Frances Blend [Elementary] School will merge with Van Ness elementary in the Larchmont area, affecting about 40 blind and visually impaired students.

Periodical and Internet Sources Bibliography

The following articles have been selected to supplement the diverse views presented in this chapter.

Tara Becker   "ACES Program Helps At-Risk Students," *Quad-City Times* (Davenport, Iowa), June 3, 2013.

Barbara Brotman   "For Valedictorian, an Emotional Culmination to Hard-Won Education," *Chicago Tribune*, June 9, 2013.

Sarah Campbell   "Alternative Programs Seek to Cut Schools' Dropout Rate," *Salisbury Post* (Salisbury, North Carolina), March 3, 2012.

Michael Alison Chandler   "Mixed-Ability Classes Attempt to Reduce Educational Stereotyping," *Washington Post*, May 17, 2012.

Laura Johnson   "Making Good: For Teens Who Want to Shift to a Positive Direction, This School Helps," *Anniston Star* (Anniston, Alabama), October 25, 2012.

Joshua Kellogg   "Alternative High Schools Provide Last Chances for At-Risk Students," *Daily Times* (Farmington, New Mexico), February 10, 2014.

Cindy Long   "Educator-Led Program Helps At-Risk Students Get to Graduation Day," *NEA Today*, December 4, 2013.

Donna St. George   "Montgomery Schools Overhauling How It Offers Alternative Education," *Washington Post*, February 26, 2014.

Joe Vaccarelli   "Denver Urban Scholars Seek More Volunteers to Mentor At-Risk Students," *Denver Post*, November 14, 2013.

OPPOSING
VIEWPOINTS®
SERIES

CHAPTER 2

What Are Alternatives to a High School Diploma?

Chapter Preface

Students often assume that if they have not received a high school diploma, or have not as an alternative taken and passed tests for a general equivalency diploma (GED), then they cannot attend college. In fact, though, many colleges will consider applicants without a high school diploma.

Jamie Littlefield, writing at About.com in an article titled "Go to College Without a High School Diploma," says that students without a high school diploma have several options available for attending college. She says that many community colleges "assume that a certain percentage of their population will apply without a high school diploma, and they plan accordingly." Such schools may even have programs targeted to help students without a diploma succeed. Littlefield adds that some colleges may allow older students who have been out of high school for a long time to enter as nontraditional students. Littlefield states that nontraditional students may be allowed "to bypass traditional requirements . . . by proving you have relevant life experience and demonstrated maturity."

A 2006 *New York Times* article, titled "Can't Complete High School? Go Right to College," states that students without a high school diploma made up 2 percent of all college students and 3 percent of community college students in 2006, for a total of 400,000 such students nationwide. By 2012 that had climbed to 836,000 students without a high school diploma or GED at two-year public colleges.

However, these numbers may soon fall. Libby A. Nelson reported in a March 20, 2012, article at *Inside Higher Ed* that federal aid for students without a high school diploma used to be available. To qualify for federal Pell grants, students without a high school diploma could take a skills test, or else could complete six college credits. However, in 2012, in an effort to reduce the federal budget, the government, "shut off both routes." Now to qualify for federal aid, a student must have a high school diploma or a GED. Nelson says that this federal decision is troubling, since part of community college's mission is to provide broad access to college. People without a high school diploma, and without a college degree, face very limited options in the workforce. Making college degrees available to those without high school diplomas, therefore, can open up opportunities and help people succeed.

The remainder of this chapter looks at other alternatives to a traditional high school diploma.

| *"On some outcomes, Hispanic dropouts with GEDs fare better than uncredentialed Hispanic dropouts."*

The GED Is a Valuable Alternative to High School for Hispanics

Richard Fry

Richard Fry is a senior research associate at the Pew Hispanic Center. In the following viewpoint, he reports that Hispanic adults with General Educational Development (GED) credentials had a higher unemployment rate than Hispanic adults who received a high school diploma. However, Hispanic workers with a GED had higher salaries than workers with a high school diploma. Fry says that the reasons for these discrepancies are not clear, but may be in part because Hispanics who take the GED are more likely to speak English. He says it may also be because Hispanic immigrants received high school diplomas from foreign institutions and US employers distrust their credentials.

As you read, consider the following questions:

1. According to Fry, why are educational prospects of Hispanic high school dropouts dimmer than others' prospects?

Richard Fry, "Hispanics, High School Dropouts and the GED," Pew Research Hispanic Trends, May 13, 2010. Copyright © 2010 by Pew Research Center. All rights reserved. Reproduced by permission.

2. For native-born Hispanic workers, who does Fry say has higher average pay, those with a high school diploma or those with a GED?

3. What benefits does the GED provide in terms of military service?

Just one in ten Hispanic high school dropouts has a General Educational Development (GED) credential, widely regarded as the best "second chance" pathway to college, vocational training and military service for adults who have not graduated from high school. By contrast, two in ten black high school dropouts and three in ten white high school dropouts have a GED, according to a Pew Hispanic Center analysis of newly available educational attainment data from the U.S. Census Bureau's 2008 American Community Survey.

Low GED Rates Among Hispanics

The relatively low level of GED credentialing among Hispanic high school dropouts is especially notable because Hispanics have a much higher high school dropout rate than do blacks or whites. Some 41% of Hispanics ages 20 and older in the United States do not have a regular high school diploma, versus 23% of comparably aged blacks and 14% of whites.

Among Hispanics, there are significant differences between the foreign born and the native born in high school diploma attainment rates and GED credentialing rates. Some 52% of foreign-born Latino adults are high school dropouts, compared with 25% of the native born. And among Hispanic dropouts, some 21% of the native born have a GED, compared with just 5% of the foreign born.

Hispanics are the nation's largest minority group; they make up 47 million, or 15%, of the population of the United States. As of 2008, there were 29 million Hispanics ages 20 and older; of this group, 41% are native born and 59% are foreign born.

This Pew Hispanic Center report also analyzes labor market outcomes of Hispanic adults based on whether they dropped out of high school, have a GED or obtained a regular high school diploma or more. Among its key findings:

- As of 2008, Hispanic adults with a GED had a higher unemployment rate than Hispanic adults with a high school diploma—9% versus 7%.

- However, Hispanic full-time, full-year workers with a GED had about the same mean annual earnings ($33,504) as Hispanic full-time, full-year workers with a high school diploma ($32,972). . . .

High School Dropouts and GEDs

Further education and training is one of the paths to upward mobility for the nation's 41 million high school dropouts. Dropouts with GEDs are much more likely to pursue postsecondary education and training than dropouts lacking a GED or other alternative credential. Among young dropouts without an alternative credential, only about 1 in 10 pursues any further education. If the dropout has a GED, about 4 in 10 get additional education. And dropouts with GEDs are the only ones who are considered for admission to degree-granting colleges and universities, including community colleges. A GED is also required to obtain the federal Pell grant [for college].

Newly available Census Bureau data reveal that Hispanic high school dropouts are the least likely of the major racial/ethnic groups to have a GED. In 2008, fewer than 1 in 10 Hispanic dropouts had a GED. Twice as many black dropouts have a GED (20%) and more than three times as many white dropouts had a GED (29%). Thus, the major racial/ethnic group having the lowest high school graduation rate from the public schools is also the population least likely to have the "second chance" credential providing opportunities for additional education.

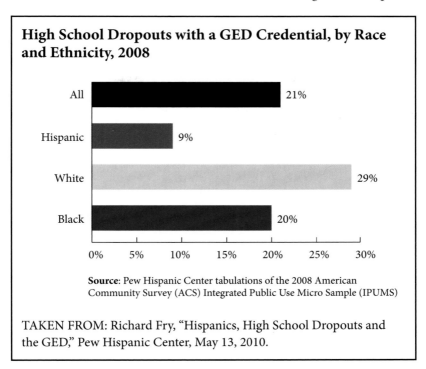

High School Dropouts with a GED Credential, by Race and Ethnicity, 2008

All — 21%
Hispanic — 9%
White — 29%
Black — 20%

(0% 5% 10% 15% 20% 25% 30%)

Source: Pew Hispanic Center tabulations of the 2008 American Community Survey (ACS) Integrated Public Use Micro Sample (IPUMS)

TAKEN FROM: Richard Fry, "Hispanics, High School Dropouts and the GED," Pew Hispanic Center, May 13, 2010.

Part of the reason that the educational prospects of Hispanic high school dropouts are dimmer than others' prospects is the large immigrant presence among Hispanic adults. The new data suggest that it takes time for newly arrived immigrants to learn about educational opportunities, including attaining GEDs. The longer Hispanic foreign-born dropouts have been in the United States, the more likely they are to have a GED. Yet, among native-born Hispanic high school dropouts, only 21% have a GED.

The GED, or General Educational Development tests, is the nation's largest dropout recovery or second chance program. Administered by the American Council on Education (ACE), the GED has standardized tests in five areas. ACE sets the minimum passing standards. States award the GED credential to test takers in their states. Some states set passing standards above the minimum, and there may be additional tests to pass (such as civics), depending on the jurisdiction. Local school districts, community colleges, correctional facilities and the military are among the major providers of GED test preparation services for dropouts.

While obtaining the GED credential opens pathways for dropouts to pursue postsecondary education, it is not clear that the GED in and of itself benefits high school dropouts. The next section shows that on some outcomes, Hispanic dropouts with GEDs fare better than uncredentialed Hispanic dropouts. In the labor market, Hispanic dropouts with GEDs may even have more favorable outcomes than Hispanics who graduated from high school with a diploma, but generally Hispanics who end their education with a GED would have been better off staying in high school and graduating.

The Value of the GED Among Hispanics

This section presents some economic and social outcomes of Hispanic adults by their highest education attained. Labor market outcomes are examined for Latinos ages 20 to 64. A few non-labor market outcomes are presented for all Hispanics ages 20 and older.

In the labor market, about two-thirds of Latinos with GEDs were employed, compared with nearly three-quarters of Latinos with high school diplomas. Hispanic adults with a GED had a higher unemployment rate (9%) than Hispanics who graduated with a high school diploma (7%). Hispanics with a high school diploma were more likely than Hispanic GED holders to be full-year workers (80% versus 75%).

Although Hispanic GED holders are less likely to have jobs and full-year work than Hispanic high school graduates, the average Hispanic GED holder may be paid more than the average Hispanic high school graduate. Among full-time, full-year workers ages 20 to 64, mean earnings for GED holders were $33,504 compared to $32,972 for Hispanics who ended their education with a high school diploma.

Why the Earnings Boost?

This is a surprising pay finding. The typical GED recipient has finished around 10 years of formal schooling, two years less schooling than high school graduates. GED examinees do invest time to prepare and pass the tests. The median GED examinee devotes 30 hours to test preparation. But in each year of high school, a student devotes 410 hours to core curriculum classes, so the typical GED holder has not invested as much time in his or her education as a high school graduate.

The higher average pay finding is found among only one group of Hispanic workers. . . . For native-born workers, high school graduates are paid more than those with GEDs. Among foreign-born workers, particularly foreign-born males, GED holders earn more than high school graduates. For example, median earnings for immigrant men who are high school graduates were $26,478, compared with $30,552 for immigrant men with a GED.

The earnings payoff to Hispanic male immigrants for having a GED rather than a high school diploma may be due to a number of factors. The male GED holders are about 2.5 years older, on average, than the male high school graduates, and they are less likely to have recently arrived in the United States. Also, although English proficiency is not a prerequisite for passing the GED tests, immigrant male GED holders are more likely than immigrant male high school graduates to be fluent in English. Fluent English speakers are paid more in the U.S. labor market.

However, it is possible that GEDs have a signaling value for male immigrants. Most of the immigrants arrived in the U.S. as adults, and those who are high school graduates received their diplomas from foreign secondary schools. Employers may have difficulty evaluating workers with foreign credentials. Immigrants with GEDs may be compensated for possessing a more familiar credential.

Standard regression analysis on immigrant male earnings reveals that the GED holders are more highly paid than high school graduates even after controlling for the differences in observable characteristics. Since these data omit some important worker characteristics, however, we can conclude only that, among Hispanic male immigrants, GEDs are associated with higher earnings compared with high school graduates.

Military and Incarceration

A benefit of the GED is that it provides an avenue to enlist in the nation's armed forces. Virtually all (99%) Hispanics on active duty in the U.S. military are either high school graduates or GED holders. So a GED seems necessary for successful enlistment. The military prefers to recruit high school graduates. Hispanics who ended their education with a GED were slightly more likely to be military veterans than Hispanics who had a high school diploma.

Hispanics whose highest education is a GED are much more likely to be currently incarcerated than are other Hispanic adults. This partly reflects the fact that correctional facilities widely provide GED preparation and testing to inmates. Though less than 1% of the population is incarcerated, more than 10% of GEDs each year are awarded by correctional facilities.

I *"The GED is not harmless."*

GED Offers "Minimal Value"

Mary Pilon

Mary Pilon is a journalist who has worked for the New York Times *and the* Wall Street Journal. *In the following viewpoint, she reports on a study suggesting that the general equivalency diploma (GED) provides minimal benefits to those who pass it in terms of salary or ongoing education. She says researchers argue that the GED may cause harm by encouraging high school students to drop out and get a GED rather than finishing a diploma and by skewing dropout statistics.*

As you read, consider the following questions:

1. According to the viewpoint, how does the GED affect the perception of African American high school graduation rates?

2. How long do GED test takers study for the exam, and how does that relate to the hours spent studying for a high school diploma?

3. Why was the GED created, according to Pilon?

Is the GED worthless?

That's a question at the heart of research from Nobel laureate Prof. James J. Heckman, and his University of Chicago co-authors Nicholas S. Mader and John Eric Humphries, in their working paper "The GED."

The GED "is America's largest high school," says Mader, one of the co-authors. "But there's substantial danger there."

The GED, shorthand for the general equivalency diploma, or general education diploma, is an eight-hour exam administered to high school dropouts to establish equivalence between dropouts who pass the exam and traditional high school graduates. In 2008, 12% of all high school credentials issued were GEDs, about 500,000 students a year.

The problem is, however, the GED is of "minimal value" in terms of labor market outcomes, the authors say, and only a handful of GED recipients use it to advance in school or the workplace. The authors cite a study that found that only 31% of GED recipients enrolled in a postsecondary institution and that 77% of those who did only stayed for a single semester.

"The GED is not harmless," the paper says. "Treating it as equivalent to a high school degree distorts social statistics and gives false signals that America is making progress when it is not." According to the paper, if GED recipients are counted as dropouts, the African-American male high school graduation rate in 2000 is approximately the same as it was in 1960.

GED recipients may face limited opportunities because they lack skills not related to the test—motivation, self-esteem, reliability, among others—to succeed in higher education and the workplace. The authors acknowledge that there are GED success stories—many smart graduates who merely lack the stamp of a traditional degree and prosper. But the gap between the GED and diploma is still wide. A quarter of GED test-takers say they spend 100 hours or more prepping for the test, which is still more than if they hadn't studied at all, but

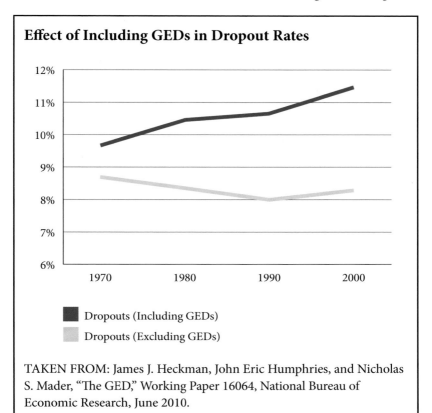

Effect of Including GEDs in Dropout Rates

Dropouts (Including GEDs)

Dropouts (Excluding GEDs)

TAKEN FROM: James J. Heckman, John Eric Humphries, and Nicholas S. Mader, "The GED," Working Paper 16064, National Bureau of Economic Research, June 2010.

the authors point out that the average high school student spends about 1,080 hours in class a year.

Because GEDs have a low cost, some students may be induced to drop out of school, the paper asserts, referencing a National Center for Education Statistics survey that found that 40.5% of high school dropouts cited that it "would be easier to get the GED" among their reasons for leaving school. Another growing share of GED takers are high school age students, says co-author Humphries. These are students who might be better off considering a traditional high school diploma or vocational program. Some states, like Virginia, pair GED programs with additional vocational or skills-development programs, which, the authors say, might better prepare students beyond the GED.

Further, GEDs may distort high school dropout rates. The exams have enjoyed more widespread usage in incarceration rehabilitation programs, meaning that a growing percentage of GEDs are now coming from the increasing prison population. With some 26% of all prison inmates earning a GED, this growth "weakens its overall signaling value by its association with criminality," the paper says. Because the gap in experience between those who get GEDs vs. those with traditional diplomas is so wide, lumping them together may be misleading.

The GED, itself, doesn't provide any additional value in the labor market, the authors say. In fact, an earlier paper co-authored by Heckman found that controlled for certain factors, that male GEDs earned on average 1% less per hour than dropouts. High school graduates made 3.6% more per hour on average than dropouts. Women GEDs earned 1.7% more per hour than dropouts and high school graduates who didn't attend college earned 10.6% more per hour. However, other research is cited in the paper that indicates that the GED can have some signaling power to employers, offering higher wages to GED recipients than if they didn't have one.

The GED was born to accommodate World War II vets, many of whom didn't complete high school before heading to war. The exam was introduced in 1942, and by 1957 civilian test-takers outnumbered veterans. The certification has boomed in recent decades, fueled in part by "government programs that promote the GED as a quick fix for addressing the high school dropout problem," the paper says, likening the GED to "wearing a broken watch and knowing that it is broken."

In general, holders of high school and college degrees have weathered the recession better than their less-educated counterparts. With rising costs of higher education, borrowing and budgets getting hit, the GED analysis comes at a profound time in education policy.

| "But adult educators . . . worry that their students, who are already beaten down and vulnerable, will give up."

A More Difficult and Expensive GED Puts a Burden on Test Takers

Kavitha Cardoza

Kavitha Cardoza is a special correspondent for WAMU, a public radio station in Washington, DC. In the following viewpoint, she says that new, more rigorous General Educational Development (GED) standards may discourage adults from getting the certification. She says that a higher price for the test, and the fact that the test is only available on computer, may put the test out of reach for many who are poor or unemployed. In addition, Cardoza reports on concerns among adult educators that there is not enough information about the transition to a new test and that they will be unable to prepare their students adequately.

As you read, consider the following questions:

1. How many adults in the United States do not have a high school diploma, and how many of them take the GED test?

2. According to Gloria Sward, why does putting the GED test on computer create barriers for her students?

3. Which states does Cardoza say are abandoning the GED test, and what are they doing to replace it?

Kiana Rucker dropped out of school when she was 15 years old to look after her younger brothers and sisters. Five years later she had a baby herself. For years, she relied mostly on food stamps, medical assistance, and subsidized housing to get by. But it always bothered her. "I don't want to rely on anyone," Rucker, now 35, says. "I don't want government help."

Opportunities

So in 2010 Rucker decided to get her General Educational Development [GED] certificate. She took classes at Southeast Ministry, a nonprofit in one of the poorest neighborhoods in Washington, D.C. This past June—three years and five attempts later—she got a phone call saying she had finally passed the GED test. "The first thing I said was, 'Are you sure you have the right person?'" Rucker says, laughing. For the first time she feels she has a future. "So many things I can do now," she says. "Go to college, get into a trade, just get a job period. Because that's the first thing they ask: 'Do you have a high school diploma or GED?' Now I can say, 'Yes, I do.'"

For Rucker and for millions of other students, the GED certificate has offered a promise of a better life, a path from poverty into college or a more promising career. Next year, though, the GED test will get much harder, and adult educators are worried that they—and their students—aren't ready for the changes.

There are approximately 30 million adults in the U.S. without a high school diploma. And almost 700,000 of them, like Rucker, take the GED test each year. "It's synonymous with a high-school equivalency for most adult education students," says Marcie Foster, a policy analyst at CLASP, a nonprofit that advocates for low-income people. "They know the acronym. It has a lot of resonance."

The GED test was first launched in 1942, as a boost to the veterans whose education was interrupted when the U.S. joined World War II. The test allowed thousands of service members to get a credential they could use to go on to college. Since then, its reach has grown dramatically. By 1958, there were more civilians taking the test than veterans. Today, it's known to some as "America's Largest High School." Thanks to government incentives, the test has become a ticket to some federal jobs programs, college grants, and, for prisoners, a chance to get out of jail a little sooner. It also has given many undocumented immigrants a better shot at staying in the U.S.

More Difficult, More Expensive

The GED test has been revised over the years, but in 2014 it will undergo a complete overhaul. It will become more difficult and more expensive. For years, the GED test was dismissively called the "Good Enough Diploma" because passing the test was so much easier than earning a traditional high school diploma. Now it's being aligned with more rigorous college and career readiness standards and will be far more difficult. Molly Broad of the American Council on Education (which along with Pearson oversees the test) says they are "raising the requirements" so the GED test will become more meaningful. To pass the new GED test, students will need some background knowledge, not just the ability to understand the passage in front of them. There will be more emphasis on critical thinking, more questions on science, and more writing. In addition, the scoring will change to identify whether the students who pass are just "high-school equivalent" or are at a new higher standard of "college- and career-ready." CT Turner with the GED Testing Service says: "If we don't provide them something of value, and they don't have the information and skills they need, we are setting them up for failure."

But adult educators estimate that changes to the GED test mean it will take a year or two longer to prepare their students. They worry that their students, who are already beaten down and vulnerable, will give up. Anthony Tassi, executive director of Literacy Partners in New York City, says these adult students have experienced a lot of change in their lives—but it's usually change being done *to* them. "They've usually been on the losing end of big bureaucratic changes," he says. "So to the extent that our students even are aware of the upcoming change, they have a lot of fear and a sense of hopelessness." Tassi and other adult educators say they are not against the change but are disappointed that there isn't more being done to prepare for the transition.

Lennox McLendon, the executive director of the National Adult Education [Professional Development Consortium], says unlike the last time the GED test underwent revisions in 2002, there has been no federal funding attached to help with the transition. He says that's because the GED Testing Service is now a for-profit entity. When McLendon organized a meeting in the spring to help states with information on the new standards, he had to raise private funds.

Concerns About the Future

Many educators also say they're frustrated because they don't know what the new test will look like. As late as April, apart from a few sample questions and some information on what will be measured, they say there were few practical resources available to help. There was no diagnostic test, no practice test and little information on accommodations for learning disabilities. McLendon says the GED Testing Service has been "late" getting information out. "It's been frustrating for local adult educators," he says.

But Turner disagrees, saying, "We have provided more information about this test earlier than we have any other GED test in our history."

The higher standards on the GED test will be paired with another change—starting next year, students will take the GED test on computers only. Pencil-and-paper tests will no longer be allowed. Students will need to know keyboarding skills such as "drag and drop," scrolling, and clicking on multiple-choice questions. Turner sees this as a sign of progress. With the online test, students will get their scores right away, instead of having to wait for months. They will see exactly which subjects they need help in. Besides, he says, you need computer skills for almost every job. "If we have an adult with a GED credential who says they are ready for the workforce and they can't apply or find a job because they can't use a computer, we haven't done our job."

Adult educators who prepare students for the GED test however, say this change will create one more barrier for their students. "Contrary to popular opinion, not every person has a computer or iPad at home," says Gloria Sward, a teacher in Palm Coast, Florida. She says most of her students don't have a computer and many don't even know what a mouse is. Steven DeMaio of Boston says, "We have about 1,000 students at the school where I teach and we only have one computer lab . . . so we can only put about five percent of our students on the computer at one time." Lecester Johnson, the executive director of Academy of Hope, an adult education center in Washington, D.C., is scrambling for money to buy more computers for her students so they can prepare for the new GED test. "For someone who doesn't have access to technology on a daily basis, we have to spend a lot of time on just the basic mechanics of using a mouse and moving around the screen," she says.

Adult educators also worry about the increased cost of the new GED test. In Illinois the price has jumped from $50 to $120, in North Carolina from $35 to $130, and in Massachusetts from $65 to $120. Turner calls the $120 price tag "rock-bottom pricing." He says states will actually save money because until now local testing centers have had to pay separately for scheduling, proctoring, and scoring the test. All of that will be included in the new price. He says that states or private employers can always subsidize the test if they choose to.

Insurmountable Barriers

But Pat Fina, an adult educator in Massachusetts, says the $55 increase is "serious money" for her students, many of whom are unemployed or struggling to get by on minimum-wage jobs. Rosemary Lischka, the director of continuing education and community services at Kansas City community college in Kansas, says the increased costs will be "insurmountable" for her students. "Many of our students buy enough gas to get where they're going on a given day and then they buy it again when they have to go somewhere else."

With all the new obstacles—the tougher standards, the computer requirement and the higher price—some states, including New York, Maine, and Montana, have decided to abandon the GED test entirely, no longer offering it as an alternative to a high school diploma. The companies CTB/McGraw-Hill and Educational Testing Service [ETS] are offering less expensive and paper-based alternatives to the GED test. Sonya Thomas, executive director of adult education and literacy for Kansas City Public Schools in Missouri, says her state has decided to dump the GED test and adopt the new ETS equivalency exam. She says students will get two free chances to retest. "That's very attractive for us. Knowing they don't have to be concerned with getting additional money together to start the whole process again if they don't pass is very important," she says.

Valarie Ashley, the executive director of Southeast Ministry in Washington, D.C., says when she was 10 years old, her mother got a GED certificate. She says it didn't take long to see the results. Her mother got a job and then a quick promotion from receptionist to office manager. "We would go to McDonald's on payday," says Ashley, "and we'd eat burgers and fries. Not only did things change in our life in terms of money, but she also started to advocate for us in school. I think it's because she felt empowered having that credential."

Now Ashley helps others, including Kiana Rucker, get their GED certificates, and like thousands of other adult educators, she is scrambling to deal with the changes coming next year. They need to hire professional teachers instead of using volunteers, buy more computers, fund-raise for IT [information technology] maintenance, and find some way to pay for the increased cost of the test. In the low-budget world of adult education, this is a huge problem. "It absolutely frightens me," says Ashley. "Will I even be able to maintain a program? I'm not trying to be like Chicken Little, but there are so many things that are unknown and unanswered. And they all have a dollar sign attached."

> "The test has to get tougher because it needs to reflect the changes that have occurred in the job market."

A Harder GED Is Coming, and It's a Good Thing for Students

James E. Causey

James E. Causey is a Milwaukee-Wisconsin Journal Sentinel editorial writer, columnist, and blogger. In the following viewpoint, he argues that a tougher General Educational Development (GED) exam will help test takers by preparing them for the competitive job market. He says that it is important for employers to know that the test actually shows that students are prepared to enter the workforce. In particular, he argues, the move to have the test on computer is vital in a current work environment where most jobs require computer skills.

As you read, consider the following questions:

1. According to Causey, what aspects of the GED testing caused so many people not to finish it?

2. Why does Causey say that the GED test needs to be challenging?

3. What did Ralph Hollmon find surprising about his visit to the Harley-Davidson plant?

The GED test will be upgraded for the first time in more than a decade in December, and some educational experts say the test will become more difficult.

The test has to get tougher because it needs to reflect the changes that have occurred in the job market. Employers are demanding more out of their workers than they did 10 years ago or even two years ago. The changes also may make a young person think twice about dropping out of school on the assumption that he or she can "just get a GED."

The original intent of the GED was to give veterans a practical way to get their high school diplomas over a short time frame. Today, close to a million people nationwide have started the GED test but haven't completed it. The current GED test contains five parts that are taken separately but must all be passed to receive a high school credential.

The current version of the test will expire on Dec. 13, and that means anyone who has not completed all of the tests by then would have to start over with the new 2014 GED.

In Wisconsin, 43,000 adults are working toward their GED, including 6,000 in Milwaukee and 9,000 in the state's correctional system. With the new test, adults who feel ready should be allowed to take all the exams in one sitting, rather than over several testing dates. I think the way the testing is set up now may be one of the reasons so many people don't complete the test.

"It would be very hard for someone to start all over, so the pressure is on them to get finished now," said Beth Lewis, alternative education and GED specialist with the state Department of Public Instruction.

There is a misconception that the GED is easy. That's not the case for someone who has been out of school for decades or more, or someone who has struggled in school before he or she dropped out.

In order to pass the GED, a person must score higher than 40% of graduating high school seniors in the United States, Lewis said.

The General Educational Development test is known in some urban areas as the *Good Enough Diploma*, but we know that for the most part it's not even good enough to get a foot in the door.

For the 1 million young people who drop out of school every year in the U.S. and for many others, earning a GED is an opportunity to get back on the right track and compete for jobs in a stagnant job market.

The new GED not only is tougher but is meant to help prepare adults for technical school and beyond, Lewis said.

In Wisconsin, adults who want to take the GED are offered free orientation at Milwaukee Area Technical College, Social Development Commission and four other sites.

Lewis said the number of people earning GEDs and signing up to take the GED and refresher courses has increased every year.

The new test will cost a bit more to take, be delivered solely on a computer, offered only in official test centers and have an essay/grammar component that may give some people problems.

The cost of the current test varies from $75 to $120 for all five tests. The new test will be $120, plus a $15 credential fee.

A harder test may be yet another roadblock to a segment of the population that does not need any more hurdles, some will argue.

But I think the test needs to be challenging because it does no good for an individual to have a certificate that's considered worthless by employers. Companies want to know if the person has the skill set to do a job.

Ralph Hollmon, president of the Milwaukee Urban League, welcomed the new test, saying that it prepares adults for the new job challenges that lie ahead.

"My mother told me a long time ago that if something is worth striving for, then you have to work harder to get it," said Hollmon, whose organization works to place many disadvantaged job seekers.

I hope the higher GED fees do not signal a cut in funding for the program for those who are incarcerated. It may be the first time that these prisoners have taken their education seriously. A majority of them will be released from prison, so it's better that they come out with a certification rather than without one.

Research has been mixed on the value of a GED. A Chicago researcher suggested that those with a GED perform at the same level as other dropouts in the labor market and other aspects of life.

I'm sure there are some college graduates who can't find a job in this economy who feel as though their degrees are worthless, too.

Hollmon said that regardless of what the research shows, it is still better to have a GED and strong soft skills than to not have them.

He recalled an incident a few years ago when Harley-Davidson called his organization looking to hire a number of people for various entry-level jobs. He said Harley required that the candidates have at least a GED. They also required the Urban League to put the candidates through a number of different tests.

"It seemed at first to be a bit much, but when I went to the plant to see for myself, it was an eye-opener. Everything in the plant was on computers," Hollmon said. "Ten years ago, that same job did not require all of those skills, but the world is changing and our workers need to be prepared."

If a harder test can help get these adults into the mind-set that much more is going to be required of them, then changing the test will have served its purpose.

Periodical and Internet Sources Bibliography

The following articles have been selected to supplement the diverse views presented in this chapter.

Christine Armario	"One in 10 Hispanic High School Dropouts Earn GED: Report," *Huffington Post*, May 13, 2010.
Stephen Ceasar	"New GED Test Stirs Competition," *Los Angeles Times*, January 6, 2014.
Michael Alison Chandler	"Those Who Opt for GED Miss Valuable Experience, Experts Say," *Washington Post*, May 13, 2013.
Eleanor Chute	"1,100 Pennsylvanians Get Credit for Passing Scores on Portions of Old GED Exam," *Pittsburgh Post-Gazette*, August 4, 2014.
James Fuller	"Fewer Students Taking, Passing New GED Test," *Chicago Daily Herald*, August 4, 2014.
Kimberly Hefling	"Test Takers Rush to Complete GED," *Huffington Post*, November 6, 2013.
Heather Hollingsworth	"Some States Dropping GED as Test Price Spikes," Associated Press, April 14, 2013.
Trey Mewes	"Time Is Running Out for Testing: GED Requirements Changing in 2014," *Austin Daily Herald* (Austin, Minnesota), December 18, 2013.
Michael Vitez	"Will Updated GED Test Help or Hurt Students?," *Philadelphia Inquirer*, December 22, 2013.

CHAPTER 3

Are Charter and Magnet Schools Good Alternatives for Students?

Chapter Preface

One of the major differences between charter schools and traditional schools is not in their educational programs, but in their labor practices. Traditional schools are usually unionized. Charter schools are generally not.

Some argue that charter schools benefit from not having unions. Jay P. Greene writing in an April 16, 2009, *Wall Street Journal* article, for example, suggests that unions create inefficiencies and needless red tape, which hurt students. He quotes Matt Lardner of the Goldwater Institute, who commented:

> "Need to change a light bulb in your classroom? Page 844, paragraph five clearly states that you must call a union electrician. You kids sit quietly with your heads down in the dark until he arrives. It will be any day now."

Along those lines, Jason L. Riley writes in a November 9, 2013, article that a charter school in New York City could not operate effectively because it was unionized. Riley says that union contracts are designed to protect teachers when they fail as well as limit what they can be asked to do. In contrast, he says, at non-unionized charter schools teachers are simply expected to promote the mission of the school, and if they do not, they can be fired. This, he says, ensures high-quality education and keeps the focus of the school on students rather than teachers.

Other writers, though, argue that teachers' unions help students, and that the move to non-unionized charters damages learning. Thus, Kristin Rawls writing at AlterNet, points out that teachers' unions protect teachers' rights to speak out for their students; without unions, teachers can be fired or silenced for pointing out administrative problems that affect students. She also argues that unions provide opportunities for professional advancement. She points to a 2002 report by

Arizona State University that, in the words of the study, "indicates higher student achievement in unionized districts."

Katrina Daneshmand, a science teacher at a charter school in Woodland Hills, California, similarly suggested that schools benefit when teachers form unions, according to a July 8, 2013, article by Tim Walker in *NEA Today*. "The teachers want input into the curriculum, calendar and school functions in order to support the students and their families," Daneshmand said. "We know what our students are capable of and we would like some say in the way our classrooms are run."

The remainder of this chapter looks at other controversies and viewpoints about alternative charter and magnet schools, focusing on such issues as whether charter and magnet schools improve student performance and whether they hurt neighborhood schools.

> *"We find that charter schools are associated with an increased likelihood of successful high school completion and an increased likelihood of enrollment at a two- or four-year college in two disparate jurisdictions."*

Charter Schools Improve High School Graduation Rates

Kevin Booker, Tim R. Sass, Brian Gill, and Ron Zimmer

Kevin Booker is a researcher at Mathematica Policy Research Inc. Tim R. Sass is professor of economics at Florida State University. Brian Gill is senior social scientist at Mathematica Policy Research Inc. Ron Zimmer is associate professor at Michigan State University. In the following viewpoint, they report on a research study in which students in Florida and Chicago charter schools had lower high school dropout rates than students in traditional schools. The authors tried to take into account self-selection, and they believe the study demonstrates that the benefit students receive is not due simply to less at-risk students choosing charters. They conclude that the benefit from charters seems to be real, though more research is needed to determine exactly why that benefit occurs.

As you read, consider the following questions:

1. Why do the authors limit their study to students who attended a charter school in eighth grade?

2. According to the authors, who did they consider to be high school graduates for purposes of this study?

3. What is one possible mechanism that the authors consider for why charter schools may have better results than traditional schools? Did their evidence support or refute this mechanism?

Charter schools have become a popular alternative to traditional public schools, with some 5,000 schools now serving more than 1.5 million students, and they have received considerable attention among researchers as a result.

Assessing Charter High Schools

Most studies focus on the effects of charter attendance on short-term student achievement (test scores), using either data sets that follow students over time or random assignment via school admission lotteries to control for differences between students in charter and traditional public schools. Beyond measuring achievement effects, however, there has been only limited analysis of the impacts of charters on the students who attend them. Even less research has been conducted on the effects of charter high schools specifically, though a large portion of all charter schools in the U.S. serve some or all of the high school grades.

Developing a high school model suited to the 21st-century student has been the Holy Grail of education reform in recent years, absorbing governors, task forces, and vast sums spent on small schools, university-based schools, and concept schools. With roughly 30 percent of American students dropping out before receiving a diploma—a rate that has been stable for several decades—assessing existing alternatives to the traditional high school is an urgent task.

In this study we use data from Chicago and Florida to estimate the effects of attending a charter high school on the likelihood that a student will complete high school and attend college. Given the impact of educational attainment on a variety of economic and social outcomes, a positive result could have significant implications for the value of school-choice programs that include charter high schools. We find evidence that charter high schools in both locations have substantial positive effects on both high school completion and college attendance. Controlling for key student characteristics (including demographics, prior test scores, and the prior choice to enroll in a charter middle school), students who attend a charter high school are 7 to 15 percentage points more likely to earn a standard diploma than students who attend a traditional public high school. Similarly, those attending a charter high school are 8 to 10 percentage points more likely to attend college. Results using an alternative method designed to address concerns about unmeasured differences between students attending charter and traditional public high schools suggest even larger positive effects. Our main results are comparable to those of some studies which find that attending a Catholic high school boosts the likelihood of high school graduation and college attendance by 10 to 18 percentage points.

Methods

Determining the influence of charter school attendance on educational attainment is difficult because students who choose to attend charter high schools may be different from students who choose to attend traditional public high schools in ways that are not readily observable. The fact that the charter students and their parents actively sought out an alternative to traditional public schools suggests the students may be more motivated or their parents more involved in their child's education than is the case for students attending traditional

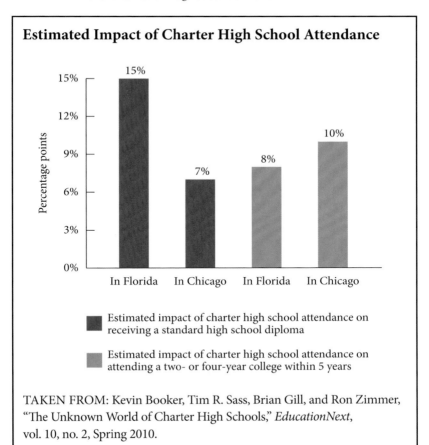

Estimated Impact of Charter High School Attendance

Estimated impact of charter high school attendance on receiving a standard high school diploma

Estimated impact of charter high school attendance on attending a two- or four-year college within 5 years

TAKEN FROM: Kevin Booker, Tim R. Sass, Brian Gill, and Ron Zimmer, "The Unknown World of Charter High Schools," *EducationNext*, vol. 10, no. 2, Spring 2010.

public schools. Since these traits are not easily measured, the estimated impact of charter high schools on educational attainment could be biased.

Our main analysis uses two methods to address students' self-selection into charter schools. First, we control for any observable differences between charter and non-charter high school students prior to high school entry. These include factors such as race/ethnicity, gender, disability status, and family income. The most important characteristic included among our statistical controls is 8th-grade test scores, which aim to capture differences in student ability and students' educational experiences prior to high school.

Second, we limit our analysis to students who attended a charter school in 8th grade, just prior to beginning high school. That is, we compare high school and postsecondary outcomes for 8th-grade charter students who entered charter high schools (the treatment group) with outcomes for 8th-grade charter students who entered conventional public high schools (the comparison group). If there are unmeasured student or family characteristics that led to the selection of charter schools in general, these unmeasured characteristics should be relatively constant among students and families who choose charter middle schools. Unlike other non-experimental studies of charter school impacts, our study therefore addresses student self-selection into charter schools directly by ensuring that the comparison students as well as the treatment students were once charter choosers.

Charter school 8th graders who went on to attend a charter high school differed from their peers who subsequently attended a traditional public high school in several respects, particularly in Florida, which suggests the importance of taking such differences into account when assessing the effects of charter attendance. However, there may still be unmeasured differences that explain why one charter 8th grader attends a charter high school while another charter 8th grader attends a traditional public high school. For this reason, we estimate charter school effects by comparing students who are more likely to attend a charter school because they live closer to one to those less likely to attend a charter school because it is less convenient. For many charter middle school students, attending a charter high school may be infeasible due to the lack of a charter high school within a reasonable distance. Such students make different choices not because of unmeasured characteristics, but because of a factor out of their control: the distance from home to the nearest charter school.

Data

The data required to analyze the impact of charter high schools on educational attainment are substantial. One must have data on school type (charter or public) and test scores of individual students prior to high school, individual-level high school attendance records and exit information, and college attendance after high school. Finally, the jurisdiction studied must have a sufficient enrollment of students in charter high schools to provide reliable results. The areas we analyze, the state of Florida and the city of Chicago, are two of just a handful of places where all of the necessary data elements are currently in place.

The Florida data, which cover the four cohorts of 8th-grade students from the school years 1997–98 to 2000–01, come from a variety of sources. The primary source for student-level information is the Florida Department of Education's K–20 Education Data Warehouse (K–20 EDW), an integrated longitudinal database covering all public school students in the state of Florida. The K–20 EDW includes detailed enrollment, demographic, and program participation information for each student, as well as reading and math achievement test scores.

As the name implies, the K–20 EDW includes student records for both K–12 public school students and students enrolled in community colleges or four-year public universities in Florida. The K–20 EDW also contains information that allows us to follow students who attend private institutions of higher education within Florida. Data from the National Student Clearinghouse, a national database that includes enrollment data on 3,300 colleges from throughout the United States, is used to track college attendance outside the state of Florida. Any individual who does not show up as enrolled in a two- or four-year college or university is classified as a non-attendee.

High school graduation is measured using withdrawal information and student award data from the K–20 EDW. Only students who receive a standard high school diploma are considered to be high school graduates. Students earning a GED [general equivalency diploma] or special education diploma are counted as not graduating. Similarly, students who withdrew with no intention of returning or left for other reasons, such as nonattendance, court action, joining the military, marriage, pregnancy, and medical problems, but did not later graduate, are counted as not graduating.

The Chicago data, which cover the five cohorts of students who were in 8th grade during the school years 1997–98 to 2001–02, were obtained from the Chicago Public Schools. The data include 8th-grade math and reading test scores and information on student gender, race/ethnicity, bilingual status, free or reduced-price lunch status, and special education status. This data set is also linked to the National Student Clearinghouse. High school graduation is determined by withdrawal information from the Chicago Public Schools data. As in Florida, only students who receive a standard high school diploma are considered to be high school graduates.

Results

The raw data on our study population of students who were in charter schools in 8th grade reveal substantial differences in educational attainment between attendees of charter high schools and those of traditional public high schools. In Florida, 57 percent of students who went from a charter school in 8th grade to a traditional public school in 9th grade received a standard high school diploma within four years, compared to 77 percent of charter 8th graders who attended a charter high school. In Chicago, the corresponding high school graduation rates were 68 and 75 percent. Similar differences are found for college attendance. In Florida, among the study population of charter 8th graders, 57 percent of students attending a charter school in 9th grade went to either a two- or four-year college within five years of starting high school, whereas among students who started high school in a traditional public school the college attendance rate was only 40 percent. In Chicago, the gap in college attendance is smaller but still sizable: among the study population of charter 8th graders, 49 percent of students at charter high schools attended college, compared to 38 percent of students at traditional public high schools.

Controlling for student demographics, 8th-grade test scores, English language skills, special education program participation, free or reduced-price lunch status (a measure of family income), and mobility during middle school does not alter the basic patterns of graduation and college attendance seen in the descriptive comparisons. The estimated impact of attending a charter high school on the probability of obtaining a high school diploma is positive in both Florida and Chicago. In Chicago, students who attended a charter high school were 7 percentage points more likely to earn a regular high school diploma than their counterparts with similar characteristics who attended a traditional public high school. The graduation differential for Florida charter schools was even larger, at 15 percentage points. The findings for college attendance are remarkably similar in Florida and Chicago. Among the study population of charter 8th graders, students who attended a charter high school in 9th grade are 8 to 10 percentage points more likely to attend college than similar students who attended a traditional public high school.

As discussed above, there remains the possibility that unobserved changes occur between 8th and 9th grade that influence both high school choice and subsequent educational attainment. For example, dissatisfaction with performance in a charter middle school that is not captured by test scores (such as discipline issues or a poor fit between the student's interests or ability and the curriculum being offered) could lead parents to choose to send their child to a traditional public high school. When we correct for this potential bias by examining students who attended charter or traditional public school based on proximity, we continue to find highly significant positive effects of attending a charter high school on both receipt of a high school diploma and college enrollment. The magnitude of the effects is large, roughly double the size of our main results.

This pattern suggests that, among students enrolled in charter schools as 8th graders, it is those who are less likely to graduate who are choosing to attend charter high schools. We can only speculate as to why this is so. It is possible that parents whose children are at risk of dropping out are more likely to choose charter high schools in a belief that the traditional public school environment would make it more likely that their child leaves school early. Alternatively, although we control for free or reduced-price lunch eligibility, it may be the case that low-income families have a stronger preference for charter schools. If so, families with children in charter high schools would be less likely to be able to afford to send their children to college.

Possible Mechanisms

The analyses reported above cannot explain how or why charter high schools appear to produce positive effects on their students' educational attainment. Our study lacks data on operations and instruction in the charter schools, so we have little opportunity to explore the mechanisms contributing to their success. Nonetheless, we have a few pieces of information that permit exploratory analyses of factors that might play a role.

First, it is worth considering that charter high schools may raise rates of high school graduation and college enrollment directly, or indirectly through improved academic achievement. We attempt to distinguish between these explanations by controlling in the analysis for math and reading achievement as measured in the 10th grade. Controlling for 10th-grade test scores explains about half the graduation differential for charter high schools in Florida but less than 20 percent of the difference in Chicago. And it has an even smaller effect on the results for college enrollment, reducing the estimated effect of charter school attendance by only about 10 percent in both locations. These patterns suggest that the positive effects of charter school attendance on educational attainment are not due solely to measured differences in the achievement of students in charter and traditional public high schools. This result is similar to those found in some studies of Catholic high schools, which suggest larger benefits for attainment than for test scores.

Second, given that charter high schools tend to be much smaller than traditional public high schools, charter school effects might simply be attributable to their smaller size. In order to assess this possibility, we ran the analyses for high school graduation and college attendance again with an additional control for the total number of students attending the school. The results are comparable to those reported above, indicating that the estimated effects of charter high schools are not due to differences in school size.

Third, we consider the possibility that the charters' success might be related to grade configurations that often differ from those of traditional public schools. In the traditional public school sector in both Chicago and Florida, high schools are almost always separate from middle schools. This is not the case for charter schools. In 2001–02, about 22 percent of charter schools in Florida offering middle school grades also offered some or all high school grades. As a result, about 30 percent of Florida charter 8th-grade students attended schools that also offered at least some high school grades. In Chicago, 40 percent of charter middle schools offered both middle and high school grades, and nearly half of the 8th-grade charter

117

students could attend at least some high school grades without changing schools. This raises the possibility that the measured effects of attending a charter high school on educational attainment could simply reflect advantages of grouping middle and high school grades together, thereby creating greater continuity for students and eliminating the disruption often associated with changing schools.

In order to examine whether charter school effects might be attributable to eliminating the transition between middle and high school, we restricted the Florida analysis to those students whose 8th-grade charter school did not offer 9th grade and ran our analyses again. For high school graduation, restricting the sample produces estimates that are nearly identical to the original estimates from our main method. Using the restricted sample and our alternative method, the estimates are about 30 percent smaller than when the full sample is employed, but still large. Meanwhile, estimates of the effect of attending a charter high school on college enrollment are even larger using the restricted sample than with the original sample that includes schools offering both 8th and 9th grade. In Florida, grade configuration is not a primary driver of the estimated positive effects of charter high schools on attainment. In Chicago, however, we could not run similar analyses because grade configuration is too strongly correlated with charter status; we therefore cannot rule out the possibility that positive results in Chicago could be partly attributable to eliminating the transition from middle school to high school.

Finally, we examined an interpretive concern arising from the fact that some charter schools in Florida are former traditional public schools that converted to charter status. If conversion schools were better-than-average traditional public schools to begin with, they may be distorting the estimated impact of charters on educational attainment. We calculated separate effects for Florida conversion and non-conversion ("de novo") charters in Florida. (In Chicago, virtually all of the charter high schools in our sample were de novo charters). We found that although Florida's conversion charters have significantly greater effects on high school graduation than do de novo charters, the impact of non-conversion charters is still sizable (nearly equal to the estimate in Chicago). For college attendance, the estimated positive impacts of Florida's de novo charters are statistically indistinguishable from the estimated positive impacts of Florida's conversion charters.

Charters Reduce Dropout Rates

Although a number of recent studies analyze the relationship between charter school attendance and student achievement, this is the first analysis of the impacts of charter school attendance on educational attainment. We find that charter schools are associated with an increased likelihood of successful high school completion and an increased likelihood of enrollment at a two- or four-year college in two disparate jurisdictions, Florida and Chicago. The reasons for these large charter school effects are not clear. There is certainly room for future work to explore how differences in curricula, expectations, peer characteristics, and other factors may cause charter schools to diminish the high school dropout rate and ease the transition to postsecondary schooling.

Our findings are consistent with some research on the efficacy of Catholic schools, which finds substantial positive effects of attending a Catholic high school on educational attainment. While just a first step, the results presented here and in the Catholic school literature suggest that school-choice programs that include alternatives to traditional public high schools may reduce high school dropout rates and promote college attendance.

> *"What started as an experiment in fixing urban education through free-market innovation is now a large part of the problem."*

Why Charter Schools Need Better Oversight

Jeff Bryant

Jeff Bryant is an associate fellow at the Campaign for America's Future and the owner of a marketing and communications consultancy serving Human Rights Watch and other organizations. In the following viewpoint, he argues that many charter schools are embroiled in real estate corruption, siphoning taxpayer money to enrich private individuals. He also says that charter schools have not been consistently superior to public schools, despite the fact that many charters kick out low-performing students to improve school scores. Bryant concludes that more regulation and monitoring of charters are needed.

As you read, consider the following questions:

1. According to Bryant, Pennsylvania's largest charter school was engaged in what corrupt practice?

2. How does Bryant say that a charter school chain in New York City manages to keep its test scores high?

3. Why does Bryant say that charter schools should be "kicking the tails" of public schools?

There are undoubtedly wonderful charter schools in existence, and Americans generally have a favorable opinion of charters, but hardly a week goes by without news of a scandal or a study tarnishing their image.

With schools reopening everywhere across the country, the past week or so was no exception in exposing new problems with an idea that was once thought of as a collaborative endeavor between teacher unions and school administrators aimed at serving struggling students, but has now become a heavily funded, well-marketed movement designed to siphon money away from traditional public schools.

Leading off the charter scandal parade was Pennsylvania, where an auditor general found that the state's largest charter school pocketed $1.2 million "in improper lease-reimbursement payments." The scheme the school was running has become all too familiar to anyone following the nefariousness of some charter school operators.

First, you take a building, "previously owned by one of the charter school's founders," according to this *Philadelphia Inquirer* story, and use municipal bonds to sell it—in this case, for $50.7 million—at very favorable terms to a "related nonprofit organization 'established for the sole purpose of supporting' the charter school." Then "the same individual who was once the charter's landlord" creates a for-profit management company to run the school. And voila, what was once a public endeavor focused on educating children for the sole purpose of raising the well-being of the community becomes a financial bonanza for a few well-placed individuals—one of whom, in this case, just happens to be "a Republican fund-raiser" who served on the governor's "transition team."

This Pennsylvania charter was no lone outlaw, as the state auditor noted. "His office had found similar problems at six other charter schools," the *Inquirer* story said.

The Aspira Trifecta Scandal

The litany of charter school scandals doesn't stop there. Philadelphia, a city that is closing neighborhood schools and leaving schoolchildren bereft of art and music teachers due to a miserly state budget, is throwing millions—a projected $729 million—at charter schools. A recent report from *Philadelphia City Paper* revealed that not all of that money spent on charters goes to educating kids.

Once again, a "nonprofit," Aspira Inc. of Pennsylvania, set up to serve the interests of charter schools, is playing a shell game with taxpayer money so a few folks get rich. Similar to other charter schemes, "millions of dollars have moved between the network of charter schools, their parent nonprofit, and two property-management entities."

Four charter schools in the Aspira chain loaned $3.3 million to Aspira "in addition to $1.5 million in lease payments to Aspira and Aspira-controlled property-management entities ACE and ACE/Dougherty, and $6.3 million in administrative fees paid to Aspira in 2012." What seems pretty clear is that Aspira has used funds from its charters to acquire real estate: The network's combined real estate holdings increased from $13.34 million in 2011 to $23.15 million in 2012. But "in the event of a default on that loan," according to the article, those real estate assets are not "at risk." Convenient, no?

Where is the school district in this affair? "We cannot conduct even limited financial audits of the parent organization," according to a district spokesperson quoted in the report. And where is the state? Noted reporter Daniel Denvir in the *Philadelphia City Paper*: "The state Auditor General, which has seen its staff reduced by 24 percent in recent years, doesn't have the capacity to audit all the new charter schools that have opened in the past five years. Only three Philadelphia charter schools have been audited since 2008. Aspira's five charters are not among them."

Cyber Scandals

Even when there's not real estate involved, charter schools in Pennsylvania find a way to make a buck at the expense of school kids. According to an article at the Raw Story, the founder of Pennsylvania's largest "cyber charter," that operates exclusively over the Internet, "was charged with fraud, for funneling $8 million of the school's funds into his personal companies and holdings." The operator, Nicholas Trombetta, "allegedly used the tax payer money to purchase a plane, houses for his mother and girlfriend, and a million dollar Florida condo."

Looking deeper into the indictment, *Crooks and Liars* blogger Karoli found that Trombetta not only headed the Pennsylvania online charter, called PA Cyber, but also set himself up as the CEO of an organization that provided curriculum and other services to online charter schools, including PA Cyber, and he created a "management group" to advise the organization he was CEO of. That's quite a trifecta.

The list of recent charter school scandals isn't confined to the Keystone State.

In Texas, a charter school located in Houston was recently accused of funneling $5.3 million in federal funds to questionable destinations, including "hotels, cruises and travel packages," six-figure salaries, and, again, a real estate scheme involving a management company and the charter school.

"Zero Tolerance" for Struggling Students

A scandal of a different kind recently enveloped another charter chain operating in New York City. In an article in the *Daily News*, reporter Juan González revealed, "Success Academy, the charter school chain that boasts sky-high student

Neoliberalism and Charter Schools

Neoliberalism is a philosophy borne out of an economic ideology that free market competition and privatization of state social services is a more efficient and effective way to run a society. Neoliberal policy makers believe that the state should not be involved in providing social services. Proponents believe that the state's role should be limited to the organization of outsourcing those services to private companies. Deregulation, tax decreases for the wealthiest citizens, opposition to unions, unrestrained capitalism, and fostering work insecurity to lower labor costs are some hallmarks of the philosophy.

In education, neoliberal policies include (a) allowing public tax dollars to be used to fund private school tuition through vouchers or tax credits to families who send their students to school outside of the public system, (b) the creation of semiprivate schools, known as charter schools, run by private companies, private boards of interested parties, or education management organizations funded by public tax dollars, (c) cutting state funding to public schools in order to foster privatization, (d) encouraging the elimination of teachers' unions in order to subvert the collective bargaining process, and (e) encouraging merit pay based on the results from one state-wide standardized test.

One result of neoliberal education policy is the creation of a two-tiered system, ripe for privatization and thus a potential cash cow for the private sector, but a loss for the common citizen and child.

Christopher H. Tienken and Donald C. Orlich,
The School Reform Landscape: Fraud, Myth, and Lies.
Lanham, MD: Rowman & Littlefield, 2013, p. 135.

scores on annual state tests, has for years used a 'zero tolerance' disciplinary policy to suspend, push out, discharge or demote the very pupils who might lower those scores—children with special needs or behavior problems."

One school in the Success chain, an elementary school, suspended 22 percent of its students at least once during the 2010–11 school year—"far above the 3% average" of other elementary schools in the district.

According to González, Success Academy chief Eva Moskowitz claimed that higher suspension rates helped achieve "order and civility in the classroom."

But high suspension rates invariably produce more school dropouts, and many states are now changing school discipline policies to reduce suspensions. Yet charter schools are often left free to determine their own discipline policies, despite the students they push out or drop out become the responsibility of other schools—or the criminal justice system.

One charter chain operating in Connecticut, Achievement First, had such high suspension rates—including "shocking numbers" of kindergartners—that a state board is now reviewing the schools' practices.

Another charter chain, Democracy Prep, has been condemned by parents of former students for its "zero tolerance" discipline policies.

Innovation for Innovation's Sake

What's apparent from all these charter school scandals is that these schools need way more scrutiny and, yes, government regulation. But the charter movement and its ardent backers in state legislatures are adamantly against that. Charters, we've been told, "need to be free to innovate."

Yet for all the "freedom to innovate" that charter schools have, the results of these schools generally fall far short of being, well, innovative.

In Ohio, a state thick with charter school "innovation" for 16 years, "charters statewide performed almost exactly the same on most measures of student achievement as the urban schools they were meant to reform," according to an article in the *Columbus Dispatch*. "And when it comes to graduating seniors after four years of high school," traditional public schools in Ohio's urban communities "performed better."

The article, written by Bill Bush, continues, "What started as an experiment in fixing urban education through free-market innovation is now a large part of the problem. Almost 84,000 Ohio students—87 percent of the state's charter-school students—attend a charter ranking D or F in meeting state performance standards."

A National Scandal

Nationwide, the statistics on charter school "innovation" aren't much better. The most recent comparison of charter school performance to traditional public schools nationwide found that more charter schools are doing better. But a careful analysis of the study showed only "a tiny real impact on the part of charter schools."

Taken into context—being freed from regulation, having the ability to select the most desirable students, implementing programs designed for test taking, having friends in high places to game the system—charter schools should be kicking the tails of traditional public schools, not barely eking out gains after years of promises and bluster.

Nevertheless, the myth of charter school magic is hard to crack.

In Louisiana, when charter schools recently failed and were closed by the state, they were replaced with . . . more charter schools. In Tennessee, the worst performing school in the state is a charter . . . protected by lobbyists. And cyber charters and other online providers in the K–12 sphere notoriously underperform traditional schools . . . but are being ramped up by policy makers in many states.

All of which denies the "first law of the hole" that the charter movement keeps digging itself—and our nation's school children—into.

What is the first law of the hole? If you find yourself in a hole, stop digging.

> "Mayor Rahm Emanuel and his pro-privatization friends want to blow up the public education system in this city."

Charter Schools Financially Starve Neighborhood Schools

Timothy Meegan

Timothy Meegan is a teacher at Theodore Roosevelt High School, a Chicago public school. In the following viewpoint, he argues that politicians and school administrators in Chicago have manufactured a public school funding crisis in order to close public schools and provide more to charter schools. He says Chicago Public Schools (CPS) is closing schools and firing teachers in order to privatize the school system. Meegan concludes that CPS is destroying the public school system that students need, and he suggests a student boycott of CPS.

As you read, consider the following questions:

1. According to the author, what is the Broad Foundation?

2. What did Secretary of Education Arne Duncan say was the best thing that happened to the education system in New Orleans?

3. How does Meegan believe public education should be run?

On Wednesday July 24 [2013], I was physically removed from a Chicago Board of Education meeting after I waited four hours to speak for two minutes. I timed it at two minutes and five seconds, but I was not allowed to finish. While board member Henry Bienen nodded off, I tried to say what I had to say: ". . .and now we are faced with budget cuts so severe that the remaining schools are left wondering how they will function at all? What the *Sun-Times* declares a conspiracy theory [editorial, July 21] is self-evident to me—that our schools are being starved into failure in order to justify mass privatization. Fifty schools closed and over 20 new charter schools [opened]. Three thousand layoffs and $1.6 million to bring in Teach for America [TFA] novices. Another $20 million on an academy for principals. All connected, along with the CEO [chief executive officer] of CPS [Chicago Public Schools], to the Broad Foundation."

Plot to Privatize

It is abundantly clear that CPS's budget crisis, underutilization crisis and now the pension crisis are manufactured to force a situation so acutely painful that the solutions of venture philanthropists will seem the only logical options. They are quietly proceeding with mass privatization against the wishes of Chicagoans and CPS parents. What may sound like a conspiracy theory to some is the reality for parents, teachers and students.

Here's the background on the folks who are trying to take over our schools—and their ties to CPS:

The Broad Foundation is a venture philanthropy (or "Philanthropic Colonialism," a term coined by Peter Buffett, son of Warren, in a recent *New York Times* op-ed), dedicated to redesigning school districts, charter proliferation and alternative teacher recruitment. Venture philanthropy is the application of business/finance principles and data-driven accountability to giving, focused on the "return on investment." Basically, venture philanthropists do not donate unless they can shape policy decisions.

To push their radical education agenda, they operate a superintendent's academy, help place their graduates and even cover a portion of their salaries. CEO [chief executive office] Barbara Byrd-Bennett led and coached for the academy, continuing that work until April 2013, even as she closed 50 schools. They also have a residency program that trains district leaders, with 13 currently working at high levels in CPS.

The Broad Foundation also finances Teach for America and the principal academy in use in CPS, called SUPES. Teach for America places new college graduates in inner-city classrooms for two years with a mere five weeks of classroom training. I expect some will replace the professional career service teachers CPS laid off. CPS funds these two programs as well, to the combined total of over $21.6 million this year, in the face of steep budget cuts to neighborhood schools.

On WTTW's *Chicago Tonight* on September 19, 2012, venture capitalist and Republican gubernatorial candidate Bruce Rauner explained the venture philanthropy agenda. Rauner declared his desire to "blow up" the district and create "smaller networks of schools competing for resources . . . through charters, contracts, and independent providers."

The Center on Reinventing Public Education (CRPE), an education privatization think tank, calls this model a portfolio district, similar to an investment portfolio. CPS has adopted that term and, last summer, CPS's portfolio office staff joined the head of the Illinois Network of Charter Schools and New Schools for Chicago for a portfolio school district meeting in Seattle. CRPE developed the student-based budgeting model CPS is putting in place this year and considers it a critical component of implementing a portfolio district.

Creating a Crisis

Mayor Rahm Emanuel and his pro-privatization friends want to blow up the public education system in this city by implementing CRPE's vision. All they lacked was the crisis to justify radical change. Solution? Make one.

First there was the bogus pretext of underutilization and mass school closures. Terms such as "right sizing" and "high quality seats" came from the Broad "School Closure Guide." The chair of CPS's Commission on School Utilization and Byrd-Bennett admitted the underutilization formula was flawed but CPS proceeded to close schools anyway.

CPS said its deficit was $1 billion. That's a lot of money. CPS has not faced an "historic" deficit like this since last year, when it was $700 million. But at the end of fiscal year they ended with a surplus of $344 million. They manufacture deficits by moving money around from one reserve to another. This year, the deficit was closed with $700 million in "reserve" funds! The entire city is facing deep budget cuts. But charter and contract school budgets are up over $85 million, while the parent group Raise Your Hand reports classroom cuts exceeding $98 million and still counting. Feast for charter/contract schools, and famine for public schools.

Secretary of Education Arne Duncan said ". . .the best thing that happened to the education system in New Orleans was Hurricane Katrina." Byrd-Bennett's colleague at the Broad Foundation Neerav Kingsland, currently CEO of New Schools for New Orleans, has laid out how to develop a portfolio district in the absence of a crisis. In "An Open Letter to Urban Superintendents in the United States of America," he advocates not for reform but "relinquishment" to independent school providers. Many of the details may be familiar to CPS parents:

". . .take over failing schools from districts and authorize new charter schools. This will give you the pressure and cover you need to be aggressive. Then rigorously approve charters.

Give the schools you do approve free facilities. Close failing schools. Repeat for five years. Then utilize alternative human capital providers to grow your talent base."

The formula for privatizing districts is the same all over the country: Open charters operated by private organizations. Simultaneously defund neighborhood schools, declare them "failing," and then close them. Fire certified professional teachers and replace them with temporary, unskilled TFA recruits.

Parents Want Public Education

But parents do not want a portfolio district. Parents want strong neighborhood public schools. We believe public education is a social service; they should be run more like a family than a business. It is wrong to operate schools as tax shelters or investment opportunities—because the profit motive distorts outcomes for children. If allowed to continue there will be no public school system in Chicago, but a system of several charter school operators whose investors will profit handsomely off of our kids. As a CPS teacher, my hands are tied. But as a parent and taxpayer, I am willing to take drastic action to save my son's public school.

Parents and students have been calling for a boycott of school this fall. Only parents can stop this madness. A school boycott will be painful for families, but I think it is worth a parent-led debate and discussion. The alternative is too costly. Once the public schools are gone, they are gone for good.

| "Charter schools are traditionally found in communities with a high concentration of minorities."

Charter High Schools Improve Outcomes for Minority Students

Jackie Hardy

Jackie Hardy is a contributing writer for the North Dallas Gazette. *In the following viewpoint, she discusses charter schools in Texas, such as the KIPP—Knowledge Is Power Program—schools. She says that minorities enroll in charters at a high rate and that charters have been more successful in promoting minority success than regular public schools have been. She says that this may be because charter schools have a freedom to innovate, which is not an option for public schools.*

As you read, consider the following questions:

1. According to Hardy, which North Texas charter schools made prestigious lists based on academic excellence?

2. KIPP schools included what percentage of minority students in the 2009–2010 school year?

3. What have been some negative stigmas associated with charter schools, according to Hardy?

According to *U.S. News & World Report*, President Barack Obama submitted a 1.35 billion dollar budget proposal to Congress in the effort to extend education grant programs for states. The Obama administration's aggressive education budget will include allocating funds for more charter schools, which operate independently of local school boards.

Creating More Charters

Charter schools are gaining national support and many states like Massachusetts are opening more charter schools in the effort to eliminate the achievement gap that low-performing public schools are experiencing typically among minority students. On the state level, Texas is also recognizing the need and importance of charter schools. Senators Dan Patrick (R-Houston) and Florence Shapiro (R-Plano) are two senators who supported House Bill (HB) 1423 that went into effect on June 19, 2009.

HB 1423 grants charters to public junior colleges for open-enrollment charter schools. Senate Bill (SB) 308, a proposed bill to lift the current 215 cap of open-enrollment charter schools granted by the State Board of Education, and SB 1830, a proposed bill to allow charters to rent space on public school ground, failed to pass in the June 2009 legislative session.

"House Bill 1423 allows community colleges to create charters in a variety of ways to either improve the college preparation of students, create schools that grant college credit and/or create schools focused on earning certifications while earning a high school diploma," explains Shapiro.

Charters and Minorities

Charter schools are traditionally found in communities with a high concentration of minorities. . . . 80 percent of minorities attend charter schools compared to 57 percent in traditional schools, thus making HB 1423 a vital legislation for minorities. This legislation can help open the door for better opportunities for minorities to attend charter schools that offer college preparatory curriculums.

"I believe the more people are exposed to the success stories about charter schools such as KIPP (Knowledge Is Power Program), Yes Prep Public Schools of Houston, and North Hills Preparatory School of Irving the sooner people will support opening more charter schools in the state of Texas, as well as see the good these charter schools are doing for our children," states Shapiro.

Three of North Texas charter schools made prestigious lists based on academic excellence. The School for the Talented and Gifted ranked fifth and the School of Science and Engineering, both at Yvonne A. Ewell Townview [Magnet] Center, ranked eighth in the 2009 *U.S. News & World Report* Best High Schools: Gold Medal List. Irving's North Hills Preparatory School, a campus of Uplift Education, which is a nonprofit and community-based college preparatory public school organization, ranked ninth in the 2009 *Newsweek* Top 1500 Best U.S. High Schools. KIPP Houston High School ranked number 16 in the same *U.S. News & World Report* list, as well.

KIPP founders Mike Feinberg and Dave Levin were two Houston inner-city elementary school teachers who witnessed firsthand the academic gap amongst minorities, which led them to start KIPP charter schools. Currently KIPP has 82 charter schools serving over 21,000 students in 19 states, including the District of Columbia.

"At KIPP, we are showing that your zip code need not determine your destiny and that college is a reality that can be achieved for all students," exclaims Steve Mancini, KIPP national spokesperson.

KIPP TRUTH [Academy] of Dallas serves a predominately African American and Latino student body. In the 2008–2009 school year, the eighth-grade class scored from the tenth to the sixtieth percentile in reading and from the twentieth to the eighty-fifth percentile in math during their four years at KIPP TRUTH. The school has also been a Recognized Campus for the past two years.

North Hills Preparatory School's largest percentage of minorities is Asians (46.1). African Americans (4.7) and Hispanics (12.7) make up less than 20 percent of its minorities. Of its graduating seniors, 93.5 percent earned at least one passing grade on the Advanced Placement (AP) or International Baccalaureate (IB) test, one attributing factor to earning a ninth rank in the 2009 *Newsweek* poll.

"Charters have the flexibility to explore innovative methods that may be better suited for a more personalized learning experience and the more types of innovation we have, the better chance we have of closing the achievement gaps," states Shapiro.

"In the 2009–2010 school year, KIPP Texas charter schools consist of 29 percent African American and 67 percent Latino. Nationally over 85 percent of KIPP's alumni have matriculated to college," states Mancini.

Charter schools are not immune to its challenges. High turnover rates and misappropriation of school funds have been some of the past negative stigmas associated with charter schools. Unlike traditional public schools that have a board of trustees and require strict compliance of district rules, charter schools do not follow district rules, but many of the charter schools like North Hills Preparatory have their own board of education.

"Being that North Hills has been around for 13 years, we have had the experience to understand how to hire teachers and leaders and develop them over time," states Laura Cobb, chief of schools for Uplift Education. "Uplift's board demands fiscal responsibility and we actually pride ourselves on the fact that we have considerably more impact on preparing our students for success in college on a much smaller cost per student than our neighboring independent school districts account for."

Flexibility

The positives seem to outweigh the negatives with respect to charter schools successfully addressing this academic gap among minorities. One possible reason is charter schools operate under a 501(c)(3) corporation status giving it the flexibility to be innovative with its teaching methods and curriculum. Many charter schools follow an AP and/or IB college preparatory curriculum(s). The IB program adopts a teaching method that promotes intercultural understanding and respect, not as an alternative to a sense of cultural and national identity, but as an essential part of life in the 21st century. "Promoting intercultural understanding helps all students to explore our country and many other countries and look at the world in a more holistic way to gain a more thorough understanding of what our responsibilities are as future citizens and leaders," states Cobb.

> "White students attending magnet schools are more exposed to low-income students than are white students in charter schools. These trends matter because ... research continues to indicate that enrollment in high minority segregated school environments is linked to harmful educational outcomes."

Magnet Schools Promote Diversity and Improve Student Performance

Genevieve Siegel-Hawley and Erica Frankenberg

Genevieve Siegel-Hawley is a research associate with the Civil Rights Project and a doctoral candidate in urban schooling at the University of California, Los Angeles. Erica Frankenberg is an assistant professor in the Department of Education Policy Studies at the Pennsylvania State University. In the following viewpoint, they summarize a number of studies that have shown that magnet schools decrease segregation and improve high school graduation rates and student achievement in areas such as read-

ing. The authors conclude that magnet schools have outper-
formed both charter schools and local public schools. They also
note that greater school diversity improves student outcomes;
therefore, when magnet schools promote diversity, they also im-
prove student achievement.

As you read, consider the following questions:

1. According to the authors, what are the benefits of attending racially and socioeconomically diverse schools?

2. What did Adam Gamoran find in his national study
   comparing magnet schools to public, Catholic, and secular private schools?

3. How do magnet school teachers compare to other teachers, according to the authors?

This research brief outlines six major studies of magnet
school student outcomes. Magnet schools are programs
with special themes or emphases designed to attract families
from a variety of different backgrounds. They were originally
established to promote voluntary racial integration in urban
districts.

The following studies are located within a much broader
body of research that documents the benefits of attending racially and socioeconomically diverse schools. Some of what we
know from the literature on the benefits of racial diversity indicates that students of all races who attend diverse schools
have higher levels of critical thinking, an ability to adopt multiple perspectives, diminished likelihood for acceptance of ste-
reotypes, higher academic achievement, more cross-racial
friendships, willingness to attend diverse colleges and live in
diverse neighborhoods, access to more privileged social networks, higher feelings of civic and communal responsibility,
higher college-going rates, and more prestigious jobs.

The research discussed here is relatively recent, but older
studies suggest that magnet schools are associated with in-

creased student achievement, higher levels of student motivation and satisfaction with school, higher levels of teacher motivation and morale, and higher levels of parent satisfaction with the school.

A Note About Magnet School Enrollment and Segregation Trends

Before delving into the research, however, we quickly review the current demographic breakdown of magnet schools. Enrollment data collected by the National Center for Education Statistics, a reliable and wide-ranging federal data set, show that, in 2008–09, more than 2.5 million students enrolled in magnet schools across the nation, up from just over two million students five years earlier. Magnet programs enrolled more than twice the number of students served by charter schools, making magnets the largest sector of choice schools.

Compared to regular public schools, both charter and magnet programs enrolled a larger share of black and Latino students (mainly due to the concentration of magnet and charter schools in more urban locales). Magnet students were slightly less likely than charter school students to attend intensely segregated minority schools, where 90–100% of students were nonwhite, and also slightly less likely to enroll in intensely segregated white schools (0–10% nonwhite students). Beyond these two extreme ends of the spectrum of white student enrollment, large differences emerged in the shares of magnet and charter students attending majority nonwhite (more racially diverse) and majority white (less diverse) schools. Forty percent of magnet students attended majority nonwhite school settings, compared to just 23 percent of charter students. Conversely, almost 35 percent of charter students attended majority white settings, compared to 20 percent of magnet students. In terms of school poverty composition, white students experience markedly lower levels of exposure to low-income students in the charter sector compared to the magnet and regular public sector, suggesting that some charters may be serving as places of white flight from poverty in other public schools. Of course, a wide diversity of school environments exists within these broad patterns for the magnet and charter sectors.

A brief comparison of the two largest choice sectors reveals that, in general, magnet school students are more likely to enroll in racially and socioeconomically diverse environments than charter school students. Further, in contradiction to concerns related to whether magnet schools "cream" more affluent students, white students attending magnet schools are *more* exposed to low-income students than are white students in charter schools. These trends matter because, as noted above, research continues to indicate that enrollment in high minority segregated school environments is linked to harmful educational outcomes, while enrollment in racially integrated schools is associated with myriad educational benefits. The following research synopsis discusses recent studies dealing specifically with the benefits associated with magnet schools.

Magnet Success in Connecticut

In a 1996 ruling, the Connecticut Supreme Court held that as a result of racial and economic isolation in Hartford and racial segregation in the 22-district region, Hartford public school students had been denied equal educational opportunity under the state constitution. The remedy called for a system of magnet schools to help bridge district boundary lines, a vital policy development since most school segregation today exists between different school districts, not within the same district. Today, the state has a system of more than 60 inter-district, regional magnet schools to help comply with *Sheff v. O'Neill*. A pair of peer-reviewed 2009 studies from Connecticut sought to examine the effectiveness of these educational settings, asking two questions: 1. Do regional magnets integrate students, and 2. what is the impact of magnet schools on student achievement?

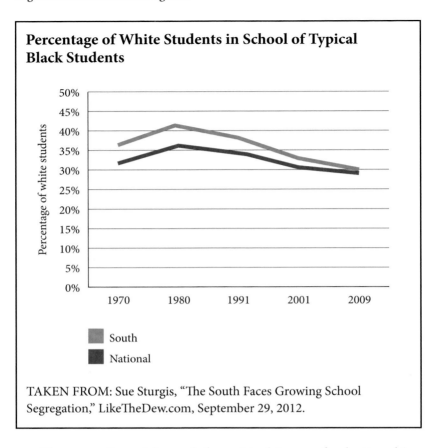

Percentage of White Students in School of Typical Black Students

TAKEN FROM: Sue Sturgis, "The South Faces Growing School Segregation," LikeTheDew.com, September 29, 2012.

These studies addressed the critical issue of selection bias, or the idea that students and families who choose magnet schools (or any other schools of choice) are fundamentally different from students and families who don't choose their educational setting, with two different sophisticated statistical methods. The research team examined magnet school lottery winners and losers, in addition to carefully controlling for pre-magnet school experiences, in order to determine the exact impact of magnet schools on achievement. Importantly, the two different methods each produced similar results, which suggested that the findings were reliable and valid.

The first article published from this research found that attendance at a regional magnet high school had positive math and reading effects for central city students, and that attendance at inter-district middle schools had positive effects on reading achievement.

The second study by the same authors found that magnet school students generally reported more positive academic attitudes and behaviors than students in non-magnet schools. These academic and social benefits of magnets included the following:

- Peer support for academic achievement was stronger in magnets than in non-magnet city schools;

- Twelfth-grade magnet city students perceived more encouragement and support for college attainment than 12th-grade city students in non-magnets;

- Magnet students were less likely to be absent or skip classes than non-magnet city students;

- Minority students in magnet city schools reported feeling significantly closer to whites and were more likely to have multiple white friends than minorities in non-magnet city schools;

- White magnet students felt more connected to minority students and were more likely to report multiple minority friends than white students from the non-magnet suburban school; and

- Magnet school students expressed stronger future multicultural interests and were significantly more likely than students in the suburban non-magnet schools to report that their school experience helped them understand people from other groups.

Together, this pair of recent studies from an innovative, inter-district magnet arrangement in Connecticut indicates improved academic and social indicators for magnet school students.

Magnets in the Nation and California

One of the more widely cited studies regarding magnet schools and achievement was published by Adam Gamoran of the University of Wisconsin at Madison in 1996. The study remains one of the few large-scale, national studies of magnet school effects.

Gamoran took a sample of urban students from the federal National Education Longitudinal [Study] (NELS) to estimate differences in 10th-grade achievement for students attending magnet schools, regular public schools, Catholic schools, and secular private schools. He also controlled for an extensive list of family background characteristics—including 8th-grade achievement. Significantly, the study showed that magnet schools were more effective than regular public schools, Catholic or secular private schools at raising student achievement in reading and social studies.

Gamoran's research supported an earlier, U.S. Department of Education (ED) study that found that over 80% of surveyed magnet schools had higher average achievement scores than the district average for regular public schools. A follow-up summary of the 1983 ED report highlighted four school districts (Austin, Dallas, San Diego, and Montgomery County, Maryland) where, after controlling for differences in student backgrounds, magnet programs had positive effects on achievement test scores.

A 2007 study out of San Diego Unified [School District], the nation's 8th-largest school system, examined the district's four systems of choice—magnets, Voluntary Enrollment Exchange Program [VEEP] (dating back to voluntary desegregation plan), open enrollment and charter schools. Both VEEP and the magnet programs contain civil rights considerations, including transportation and outreach; and the study found that they produced more racial integration than the other two systems of choice. Beyond magnet schools' ability to foster diverse learning environments, the authors found that winning the magnet lottery at the high school level increased math achievement two and three years after entering the program, which the authors suggest is likely a causal relationship (in other words, magnet schools caused math achievement effects).

Another California study looked at magnet programs in Los Angeles Unified [School District (LAUSD)], the second-largest district in the nation. As early as 1982, school desegregation in Los Angeles was limited almost entirely to a system of magnet schools. Nearly three decades later, in 2008, UCLA [University of California, Los Angeles] researchers tracked the individual data records of 48,561 students through their high school experience. After controlling for a variety of student-level factors (like race, gender and absenteeism) and school-related factors (magnet or non-magnet, poverty and racial concentrations, teacher quality), the research team found that students enrolled in LAUSD's magnet programs graduated at *much* higher rates than non-magnet students. Specifically, 73% of students attending a magnet high school in the district graduated, compared to 43% of non-magnet students. Stated differently, attending a magnet more than doubled the probability of a student earning a high school diploma.

Magnets Create Diversity and Success

Finally, a new study using an econometric analysis of long-term outcomes for magnet schools in a mid-sized urban school district led researchers to conclude that "magnet programs are effective tools for attracting and retaining households and students." By carefully analyzing the impact of winning or losing the magnet school lottery, as well as decisions to stay or leave the school district, the team of researchers found that magnet schools were able to retain significant groups of white students from higher income and more highly educated communities. The data also indicated that students in the district's high school magnet programs had better at-

145

tendance records than non-magnet school students. The first finding is extremely significant, since it suggests that magnet schools are continuing to carry out their original mission.

Teaching is strongly related to student outcomes—indeed, teachers are the most predictive school factor related to student performance. We also know that stability and experience of teaching faculties is critical. Importantly, a Civil Rights Project study found that magnet school faculties are more stable than non-magnet school faculties, in addition to being more racially diverse. Further, another Civil Rights Project study on the Clark County/Las Vegas school district found that magnet schools were more successful in retaining experienced teachers than non-magnet programs in the district. Again, these findings are situated in a larger body of work documenting the exit of experienced and highly qualified teachers from schools that are resegregating by race and socioeconomic status.

> *"Funding for magnets is based on a dizzying hodgepodge of financial arrangements that perplex educators, pit towns against one another, and stir a chorus of protest."*

Funding of Connecticut Magnet Schools Is Unfair and Unsustainable

Robert A. Frahm

Robert A. Frahm is the education reporter for the Connecticut Mirror. *In the following viewpoint, he reports that magnet school funding in Connecticut is convoluted and is damaging the state's budget. A 1996 ruling by the state supreme court demanded that Connecticut reduce segregation in Hartford's city schools; magnets were developed to meet that obligation. However, magnet school funding in the state has been complicated, and in many cases, requires the state to pay double for each student who goes to a magnet. Especially since the 2008 financial crisis, these payments have become less and less sustainable. Frahm concludes that Connecticut does not know how to fund magnet schools for the future.*

Robert A. Frahm, "Magnet School Costs Strain State, Local Budgets," *Connecticut Mirror*, January 26, 2010. Copyright © 2010 by Connecticut Mirror. All rights reserved. Reproduced by permission.

As you read, consider the following questions:

1. According to Frahm, when did the issue of magnet school funding boil over in Connecticut?

2. What is the average annual cost of magnet schools per pupil, and how does that compare to not-magnet schools in Connecticut?

3. What changes to school funding were recommended by ConnCAN?

As parents strolled among rows of displays at a recent magnet school fair in Hartford, those who stopped at a booth for the city's Classical Magnet School heard an appealing sales pitch.

Tim Sullivan, the school's high-energy principal, told them about the prep-school atmosphere at Classical Magnet, a place where college-bound teenagers study Latin, read Shakespeare and put in long hours of homework.

"Private school quality at a public school price," he said.

Free Is Expensive

The prospect of a free, high-quality education has obvious appeal for parents and students hoping for a spot at one of Connecticut's many public magnet schools, but the rising cost of running these popular, specialized schools is raising new disputes over how to pay for them.

Magnet schools such as Classical, drawing a racially mixed student body from cities and suburbs, have been the key strategy in Connecticut's effort to comply with the *Sheff v. O'Neill* court ruling on school desegregation in Hartford. Now, however, their cost—combined with the state's worsening financial crisis—has pushed state and local education budgets to the brink.

Funding for magnets is based on a dizzying hodgepodge of financial arrangements that perplex educators, pit towns against one another, and stir a chorus of protest. Some magnets charge tuition to the hometowns of non-resident students while others do not. In some cases, the state pays two different school districts for the same students. Under pressure to comply with the *Sheff* order, the state pays larger subsidies to Hartford-area magnets than to magnets outside the region.

"The whole system is broken," says state education commissioner Mark McQuillan.

The issue boiled over last year [2009] when Hartford Superintendent of Schools Steven Adamowski sent tuition bills to suburban towns whose children attend Hartford magnets such as Classical, threatening to throw out students whose hometowns refused to pay. Later, he also threatened to refuse to pay for busing suburban students to Hartford.

The legislature stepped in, raising state subsidies for Hartford magnets, forbidding the city to charge tuition, and providing an emergency subsidy for busing. But educators say the problem is not fixed. Suburban officials, who still must pay tuition for other regionally operated magnets supporting the *Sheff* case, have been hit with larger than expected tuition bills this year. Adamowski, meanwhile, says the spiraling cost calls for an overhaul of the state's strategy for magnet schools under the *Sheff* ruling.

"There's a need for *Sheff* reform," he said. "You can't viably do this under the current system because it's so expensive."

The *Sheff* Ruling

The 1996 ruling by the state supreme court—ordering Connecticut to reduce the level of racial segregation in Hartford's mostly black and Hispanic school system—led to an explosion in the growth of magnet schools with popular themes such as science, mathematics and the arts. When the legislature passed a law in 1996 promising to pay the full cost (later reduced to 95 percent) of building new magnets, the specialty schools sprouted not only in Hartford but across the state. In the

1995–96 school year, there were just eight magnet schools in Connecticut with about 1,500 students. Today, there are 61 magnets enrolling nearly 22,000 students.

Over the past two decades, the state has approved nearly $2 billion for dozens of magnet school construction projects, including more than $700 million for schools designed to meet the *Sheff* order in the greater Hartford region. That includes schools such as Classical, built for about $36 million, and Hartford's Sport and Medical Sciences Academy, a state-of-the-art building that opened in 2008 for nearly $72 million.

With features such as extra arts or music programs, the latest technology, longer school years and lower class sizes, magnet schools also cost more to run than most other schools. An analysis of state data shows an average annual cost of $12,845 per pupil at *Sheff*-related magnets in the greater Hartford region, about $2,500 more than the overall statewide average for public schools.

Last fall, as the legislature finalized the state budget, lawmakers called for a halt on new magnet school construction outside of the *Sheff* region and ordered the state department of education to develop a comprehensive statewide magnet school plan by next January.

"There's been a real growth spurt in magnets, and it's probably a good time to take a breather," said state senator Thomas Gaffey, D-Meriden, co-chairman of the legislature's education committee.

Complex Funding

As the number of magnet schools grew, so did a piecemeal approach to funding them. The financial formulas are so numerous that even many educators do not understand them, says David Title, superintendent of schools in Bloomfield. "I do not think there is a more complex and misunderstood topic," he wrote in a recent paper summarizing the issue.

Hartford and Segregation

In 1970 ..., a group of local attorneys working for the local NAACP [a civil rights organization] had filed a class-action lawsuit in federal district court on behalf of racial minority families in Hartford. The complaint, *Lumpkin v. Meskill*, had charged that the state maintained segregated schools in violation of the U.S. Constitution. Two years later, the city of Hartford itself had filed a similar complaint.

The first constitutional violation, according to *Lumpkin*, was that Connecticut—like most Northern and Midwestern states and unlike much of the post-*Brown* [*Brown v. Board of Education*, a desegregation decision] South—had established each town or city as a separate school district and required students to attend school where they lived. "Numerous" schools within Hartford, the lawyers had pointed out, had minority group enrollments "in excess of 90 percent." Soon, the lawyers contended, desegregating schools within Hartford's borders would be futile. A true remedy to segregation, *Lumpkin* asserted, would fold suburban communities into a regional desegregation plan, a configuration that had become common and no longer novel or controversial down South. Lawyers suggested starting with two contiguous municipalities: Windsor and West Hartford.

Susan Eaton, The Children in Room E4:
American Education on Trial. *Chapel Hill, NC:
Algonquin Books of Chapel Hill, 2007, p.79.*

Consider, for example, the two different methods of funding of magnet schools in the Hartford region. Some are part of the city school system while others are operated by the Capitol Region Education Council, a regional agency known as CREC.

The city's magnets, such as Classical, operate under the city budget but get a $12,000 stipend from the state for each suburban student they enroll. The CREC magnets get $9,695 per student from the state but can charge tuition to local districts to make up the remaining cost of running the schools. With state funds limited, tuition at many of those schools rose sharply this year, ranging from $2,517 to $4,950 per student.

Because school districts cannot control tuition or limit the number of students who choose magnets, the schools are "potential financial money pits," Title wrote.

In Bloomfield, where one of every six students left the district to attend magnet schools this year, the tuition to CREC magnets was at least $100,000 more than anticipated, he said.

Some critics complain that magnet schools in the *Sheff* region get more attention than others do—and more money.

This year, for example, while CREC and Hartford received increases in magnet school subsidies, other magnet schools did not. Regional agencies outside of Hartford got about $2,000 less per student in state magnet payments than CREC received. And when Hartford threatened last fall to end busing for suburban magnet students coming to city schools—a move that could have undermined requirements of the *Sheff* ruling—the state agreed to come up with an emergency grant.

"I want to find out how Hartford got $3 million just by saying they couldn't afford the buses," Pat Perugino, chairman of the Plymouth Board of Education, said at a recent statewide convention of superintendents and school boards.

Adding to the cost of magnets is a provision that requires the state to pay twice for many magnet students. In addition to paying a subsidy to the magnet schools, the state continues to count magnet students in the formula for state aid to local districts even though they no longer attend their hometown schools.

State school aid can range from a few hundred dollars per student in wealthier suburbs to thousands of dollars per student in the state's poorest cities.

Adamowski, the Hartford superintendent, says that paying two different school districts for magnet students "is terribly bad public policy." A New Britain student attending Hartford's Classical magnet, for example, costs the state $12,000 in the magnet subsidy, $1,400 in busing costs and counts for another $6,733 in New Britain's state aid formula—more than $20,000 in all.

Some critics, including Adamowski, favor a system that would eliminate double payments by linking state aid directly to each student, sending the money to whatever school the student attends—a magnet, a charter, a technical school or the local neighborhood school, for example. That idea—allowing the money to follow the student—is the central recommendation in a recent report by the New Haven–based school reform group ConnCAN. The report recommends giving added weight to needier students—those who speak limited English or come from low-income families.

Because the plan would produce winners and losers—bolstering aid for some schools while reducing support for others—it undoubtedly would be controversial.

"It would cause a political eruption in the state," said Gaffey, the education committee co-chair. "I just don't see it happening."

Financial Squeeze

Much of the angst over funding formulas can be traced to the mounting financial squeeze on state and local budgets, and Gaffey said the issue won't be resolved this year "considering the dire straits right now."

He said, "The hope for more money is like a pipe dream."

Nevertheless, nearly everyone agrees that some type of reform is needed to change a magnet school funding process that many believe is unfair.

When Adamowski, the Hartford superintendent, sent letters last year threatening to charge tuition to suburbs or deny enrollment to their students, "kids and families were the pawns," said Elizabeth Feser, superintendent of schools in Windsor. "That was the most disheartening thing. . . . That whole scenario eroded trust toward the whole magnet school piece."

Cal Heminway, chairman of the Granby Board of Education, said, "The patchwork of funds is setting towns against towns, and that is a huge mistake."

Against the backdrop of a state budget now awash in red ink, the prospects for a solution remain bleak.

Heminway said he would like to see school officials from Hartford and suburban towns meet with *Sheff* plaintiffs and state legislators to discuss the problem. But, he added, "I don't think the legislature has a clue as to where they're going to get the money for just about anything."

Periodical and Internet Sources Bibliography

The following articles have been selected to supplement the diverse views presented in this chapter.

Arizona Daily Independent	"TUSD's Magnets Are Attracting Criticism Not Students," February 20, 2012.
Gregory Kane	"Gregory Kane: Charter Schools Don't Work? Results Say Differently," *San Francisco Examiner*, June 21, 2010.
Patti Neighmond	"High-Performing Charter Schools May Improve Students' Health," NPR, July 21, 2014.
Gary Orfield	"Magnet Schools Are an Important Option for LAUSD," *Huffington Post*, December 20, 2011.
Clarence Page	"Clarence Page: Failing Charter Schools Hurt Reputation of Successes," *Houston Chronicle*, July 1, 2010.
Motoko Rich	"Magnet Schools Find a Renewed Embrace in Cities," *New York Times*, February 16, 2014.
Valerie Strauss	"Charter Schools That Start Bad Stay Bad, Study Finds," *Washington Post*, January 31, 2013.
Carolyn Thompson	"Charter Schools Benefit Minorities, Poor Families Most, Study Shows," *Huffington Post*, June 25, 2013.
Maria R. Traska	"The Void in Charter Schools," *American Libraries*, June 2013.
Jed Wallace	"When Charter Schools Fail, Close Them," *Los Angeles Times*, December 23, 2013.

CHAPTER 4

Is Online Learning a Good Alternative for High School Students?

Chapter Preface

Online learning has opened up opportunities for adult high school dropouts to return to school and obtain a diploma.

Sandra Ransel, the principal of alternative high school Desert Rose in Las Vegas, writes about the importance of high school opportunities for adults in a February 2010 article in *Educational Leadership*. Ransel notes that high school dropouts earn $250,000 less over a lifetime than do high school graduates, a substantial difference that can put their children at risk of poverty. Ransel adds that adult students returning to school have special needs, including continuous enrollment and flexible schedules. Thus, she says, "We make certain classes—such as health and American government—available as independent studies or online so that students can complete course work at home, with teacher guidance, and take the necessary tests in school."

Other schools are taking even more advantage of online learning opportunities. For instance, Amy Huddleston in a June 15, 2011, article in the *Twin Falls Times-News*, reports on the iSucceed Virtual High School, which was founded specifically to help Idaho high school dropouts pursue a diploma. Huddleston interviewed Destanie Breland, a student who dropped out of school after becoming pregnant at eighteen. Breland, who graduated from iSucceed, told Huddleston, "I want to show my daughter when she is older that even if you get divorced, pregnant or move to another state, you can still finish school if you put your mind to it." Breland says she appreciated the program's flexibility, which allowed her to study at night and to continue schooling throughout her pregnancy.

Julie Watson in a January 9, 2014, article for the Associated Press writes about another online program for high school dropouts, this one based in the Los Angeles Public Library. The library partnered with a private online learning company; students take courses online, but meet at the library to talk to fellow adult students and get assistance. According to Watson, the library hopes to grant 150 diplomas in its first year at a cost of roughly $150,000. Library director John Szabo said that the partnership should work in part because "the exciting thing about public libraries is they are places people trust. . . . So people, who may have felt ashamed about not having a high school diploma, will feel safe going there to get one."

The remainder of this chapter looks at other possible ways in which online learning may be used as an alternative to traditional education methods.

> *"While the [distance education] context makes communication, interaction, and relationships more important, it also makes them more difficult in many ways."*

Motivating High School Students in Online Courses Is Difficult

Elizabeth Murphy and María A. Rodríguez-Manzanares

Elizabeth Murphy is associate professor and María A. Rodríguez-Manzanares is a doctoral candidate in the Faculty of Education, Memorial University of Newfoundland. In the following viewpoint, they report on a study they did of online learning teachers in Canada. The teachers reported that motivating students in online classrooms is more difficult than motivating students in a face-to-face (F2F) setting. The authors suggest a number of ways to improve student motivation based on their interviews. These strategies include accessible teaching styles, interactive course structures, and the use of lessons that are engaging and use multimedia elements.

Elizabeth Murphy and María A. Rodríguez-Manzanares, "Teachers' Perspectives on Motivation in High School Distance Education," *Journal of Distance Education*, vol. 23, no. 3, 2009. Licensed under CC by 3.0.

As you read, consider the following questions:

1. According to the authors, why might young distance education students face special challenges in online learning?

2. What do Lim and Kim say is the weakest aspect of on-line instruction?

3. Name three recommendations that the authors make for learner-centered design.

Motivation in distance education (DE) has been studied mostly at the postsecondary level with few studies having been conducted at the high school level. This [viewpoint] breaks with this tradition by reporting on the perspectives on motivation of 42 Canadian high school DE teachers. Data collection involved one-hour long, semi-structured telephone interviews across the eastern, central, and western areas of the country. . . .

Difficulties in Motivating Students in DE

Motivation is one of the most significant components of learning in any educational context. It has been identified as a determinant of student satisfaction and perceived learning outcomes in distance education (DE) environments. While motivation is critical for student success in DE, it is not always easily promoted. A lack of nonverbal and nonvisual cues may hinder communication, and students may feel socially isolated. They may have little or no supervision, and some students may procrastinate. Lack of motivation has been identified as a cause of student attrition in DE.

In general, motivating students in DE contexts is challenging especially in cases where interaction is low, such as in self-directed online instruction. Motivating young DE students poses special challenges. As [R.] Smith et al. argued, young students might have less autonomy and independence than adult students as well as less intrinsic motivation "to help them persist in their studies." DE learners need to manage their learning, monitor their work, and be self-directed, all of which can be challenging for young students.

Motivation in DE has been studied mostly at the postsecondary level, with few studies having been conducted at the high school level. In general, according to Smith et al., high school DE has not yet received extensive attention compared to the postsecondary level. At the kindergarten to grade 12 (K–12) level, there is comparatively less research on student motivation than on other issues such as implementation. In addition, the research conducted to date on motivation in DE has focused on motivation from the student's perspective, but comparatively less attention has been paid to teachers' perspectives on motivating high school DE students. As [J.C.] Turner indicated with respect to research on motivation in general, "the focus . . . should move beyond students alone." In this [viewpoint], we report on a study of Canadian high school DE teachers' perspectives on motivation. We begin with a literature review that focuses specifically on motivation in DE environments. . . .

Methods

The findings presented in this [viewpoint] are part of a larger data set collected in a study of teachers in high school DE classrooms. Forty-two teachers were recruited as follows: 11 from western Canada, 21 from central Canada, and 10 from eastern Canada. Our selection was driven by an interest in representing a diverse range of perspectives from across the country. All teachers who consented to participate were included. The teachers worked from different locations, including physical schools, offices, and their home. They worked for a total of 14 different organisations, such as virtual schools, regional or district school boards or divisions, or learning units working directly under a provincial department of education. Only one of the teachers worked at a private institution. All others were employed by a public school system. Of the 42 teachers, three had previously taught in a context of correspondence distance education and one in a context of videoconferencing. The remaining 38 teachers had between one and 10 years of experience teaching in an online setting.

We conducted semi-structured, one-hour long telephone interviews with the 42 teachers in May and June of 2008. The questions related to motivation were as follows: In what ways do you motivate or engage students?; How do you know if your students are motivated and engaged?; In what ways is motivating and engaging your students different or similar to motivating them F2F [face-to-face]? These open-ended questions were supplemented in the course of the interviews by additional probing questions to gain deeper insights. . . .

Communication, Interaction, and Social Presence

Teachers' perspectives contrast, on one hand, the personable, real-time, individual connection and communication that occur normally in F2F contexts with the depersonalized computer or "robot" behind the screen on the other. In DE, individuals have to be able to "project themselves affectively within [a] medium" ([D.R.] Garrison, 1997, p. 6). As Garrison also indicates, this may be done verbally or nonverbally. In an environment without visual cues as in DE, students may feel isolated. Teachers' affective projection is, therefore, important. Tone of voice, humour, personal relationships are part of this projection. Garrison, [T.] Anderson, and [W.] Archer described social presence as "the ability of participants . . . to project their personal characteristics into the community, thereby presenting themselves to the other participants as 'real people.'" Humour is an indicator of social presence and is part of "socio-emotional communication" necessary in online learning.

Humour, together with self-disclosure and expressions of emotion, are ways of displaying affect in computer-mediated communication which [L.] Rourke, [T.] Anderson, [D.R.] Garrison, and [W.] Archer identified as indicators of social presence. In a study of social presence in the web-based synchronous high school classroom, [N.] Nippard and [E.] Murphy identified the following social presence indicators: use of humour; use of informal language to show affection; and teacher self-disclosure. In a postsecondary context, [D.] Lim and [H.] Kim's study of motivation in online learning found that, although emotional involvement and relationships were important in terms of motivating students, they were not always easy to achieve: "The weakest aspect of online instruction has been said to be the lack of instructor student relationship through 'eye to eye' and 'tongue to tongue' communication that creates online learners' emotional involvement in the learning process."

In their study of high school DE, [E.] Murphy and [M.] Rodríguez-Manzanares observed findings similar to those of Lim and Kim. In the DE classroom, teachers cannot typically interact physically or F2F with students. Informal, off-chance, casual social interactions outside of class and in corridors are not possible. Personal interactions and rapport building must be "premeditated," "consciously promoted" and "can only be achieved with more work."

[M.G.] Moore argued that, in DE, the greater the transactional distance, or the "space of potential misunderstanding between the inputs of instructor and those of the learner," the more autonomy the learner has to exercise. He defines learner autonomy as "the extent to which in a programme the learner determines objectives, implementation procedures, and resources and evaluation" and opposes it to teacher control. Murphy and Rodríguez-Manzanares hypothesised that synchronous classes might help compensate for the lack of self-motivation and self-direction of some students at the high school level. Transactional distance could also be decreased by "deliberate strategies to promote rapport, collaboration, and engagement."

[L.] Liao's emphasis on the importance of learner-teacher interaction as opposed to learner-learner interaction was confirmed by teachers' perspectives in our study. These perspectives suggest that teacher-student interaction may serve as what [B.] Tuckman referred to as a motivational scaffold. The perspectives provide insight into the forms that interaction might take in high school DE. Interaction in this context goes beyond simply talking to students and includes developing rapport and personal relationships, communicating in real time, and even visiting students F2F. While interaction may be important, teachers' perspectives also highlight the difficulties associated with interaction including communicating the correct tone, ensuring that feedback is positive, and encouraging students to communicate. . . .

How Teachers Can Motivate Students

The findings reported in this [viewpoint] add to the literature on motivation in high school DE by shifting attention away from issues of students' self-efficacy, self-regulation, and self-motivation to the specific role that teachers can play in motivation in this context. As we noted at the beginning of this [viewpoint], students at the secondary level are less likely to be autonomous and independent than would be postsecondary students. They may lack intrinsic motivation and be less able to manage their learning, monitor their work, or be self-directed. For these reasons, the high school DE teacher has a pivotal role to play in promoting motivation in this context. Our study suggests numerous techniques and strategies that teachers might use for this purpose.

The study was limited to use of interviews only. A variety of data-collection techniques such as observations of DE students and teachers could have provided additional insights.

Motivation and Dropping Out

When distance students who have dropped out of distance education are asked why, they give a wide range of answers—usually time problems, frequently job and family issues, sometimes illness, bereavement and so on—and undoubtedly many of these reasons must be right. But there are students who have experienced the most severe problems but have kept going, and practically all the same reasons must apply to part-time students, whose dropout rates are far less. . . .

I suspect that in the end what drives most students out of distance education is loss of the motivation to learn, whatever the activating event that finally tipped the balance. Students who can maintain that motivation can succeed under the most extraordinary difficulties. Almost anyone who has worked in distance education has stories of students who have overcome the most horrendous personal, family and other problems because they were determined to complete their studies.

Indeed, I would argue that motivation is not only a necessary condition for success but is often also a sufficient one. A learner who is fully motivated will overcome barriers of situation and time, find ways of developing appropriate skills and be able to deal with the stress of study with very little extra external support, and will become that most desirable of distance students—the "independent learner."

Ormond Simpson, Supporting Students for Success in Online and Distance Education. *3rd edition.* New York: Routledge, 2012, pp. 76–77.

We were concerned with DE in Canada only. Had we included teachers from the United States, where there exist a number of virtual high schools and cyber schools, our findings might have been different. The fact that the participating teachers worked for different organisations with different approaches to the delivery and design of high school DE prevented us from drawing definitive conclusions. In-depth case studies of particular DE organisations with similar approaches to, for example, percentages of asynchronous and synchronous delivery would likely provide more insight into factors affecting motivation in high school DE.[1] The scope of our study did not allow us to investigate specific characteristics of DE delivery models in relation to student motivation. Based on our findings, we can only hypothesise that issues related to high school student motivation might manifest themselves differently in synchronous versus asynchronous DE and, therefore, place different demands on teachers and require different emphases in their practices. Studies of delivery models such as asynchronous versus synchronous and their relation to student motivation could prove valuable in terms of informing policy.

In terms of practice, our findings suggest that, as in a F2F context, communication, interaction, and relationships were important in terms of motivating students. However, in the DE environment, they take on an added importance because individuals are separated in space and, often, in time. While the DE context makes communication, interaction, and relationships more important, it also makes them more difficult in many ways. Organizational or policy decisions may need to take into careful consideration the types of learning management systems and tools being used to support learning in these contexts. How well do they support, for example, communication, interaction, feedback, and not solely tracking and monitoring?

---

1. In synchronous learning, all students are present at the same time, through, for example, a web conference. In asynchronous learning, students interact with course material on their own schedule.

Our findings point to the potential value of professional development opportunities to identify strategies and techniques to promote communication, interaction, and relationships in the DE high school classroom. Techniques and strategies to promote communication, interaction, and social presence are summarized as follows: . . .

- Communicate one-on-one with students.

- Ask personal questions.

- Maintain a sense of humour.

- Make assessment tools more "fun."

- Have a phone conversation with students so that they can recognize the teacher's voice.

- Monitor students' tone of voice of their written messages.

- Use a motivating voice.

- Where possible, hold a face-to-face meeting with students.

- Provide detailed, quality, frequent, and prompt feedback.

- Put marks into perspective in assignments.

- Be very careful in phrasing feedback.

- Establish initial contact and open the lines of communication with students.

- Identify students' strengths and interests.

- Engage in real-time communication with students.

- Offer help when students are struggling.

- Send invitations when students drift away.

- Rely on communication to read between the lines.

- Help students associate a face with the teacher.

- Teach students to communicate any frustration.

- Look for indicators of whether students are motivated.

- Interact with students on a daily basis and keep them involved.

- Use a discussion board for personal greetings at the beginning of a course.

- Use a news forum which becomes the first thing students are supposed to look at in the morning.

- Use assignments that require students to contribute and respond to each other's ideas.

- Center discussions on controversial issues so that students have to provide their opinion.

- Provide opportunities for students to participate in a chat.

Policies for Motivating Students

Likewise, teachers may need to develop approaches to and awareness of both intrinsic and extrinsic ways of motivating students in these contexts. Organizations delivering DE to high school students may wish to develop plans of action to identify and support students who might have low levels of intrinsic motivation. Local facilitators and parents may have an important role to play in this regard. Policy implications may include the need to hire additional personnel such as DE guidance counsellors who can support at-risk or unmotivated students. Specific strategies and techniques related to these forms of motivation are as follows:

- Use a student-tracking program to monitor presence or pages visited.

- Use student checklists to keep students engaged.

- Use an attendance structure.

- Ask students to use tools (e.g., a message board) a certain amount of times.

- Convey the idea that distance learning is just like regular school.

- Assign marks for participating in discussion forums, accessing course materials, or submitting work by a certain time.

- Use contests, prizes, points, and money for scholarships to encourage participation.

- Use formative assessment tasks.

- Allow students to resubmit assignments and reward the resubmission with a higher mark.

- Emphasise the importance of independent work and study skills.

- Use a screening process and readiness quizzes to see if students are actually ready to be independent and work within time-management guidelines.

- Involve parents by sending them letters or copying them in e-mails.

- Rely on school facilitators to motivate students and act as a liaison.

- Rely on the school's guidance counsellor if students don't keep up with their work or if they are struggling.

- Use encouraging comments in e-mails.

- Encourage students to look at a distance course as a series of small steps.

- Help students set weekly goals.

- Include lower stakes before higher-stakes assessment activities.

Learner-Centered Designs

The importance of the design of learning suggests that specific multimedia skills will be required by teachers in order to promote learner-centered designs that move away from simple emphasis on text. The inclusion of more multimedia may have policy implications since they may require not only more bandwidth but, as well, the hiring of instructional designers and graphic artists. In cases where DE programs are intended to provide equal and quality educational opportunities for all learners, such as in contexts of public schooling programs in DE format, their design may need to take into account the diversity of learners in terms of their motivation. We have summarised the specific strategies and techniques related to design as follows:

- Move beyond monotonous text to meet different learning styles.

- Add interactivity and visual appeal.

- Instead of question/answer type assignments, rely on data manipulation or image interpretation.

- Use online as opposed to printed quizzes that provide instant results.

- Make assignments worth students' time and effort.

- Use more multimedia-based assessment.

- Strip extra information and include only the essentials.

- Use social networking tools and videos.

- Provide tutorial videos.

- Adjust timelines so that when students check their marks they are reminded about deadlines.

- Provide students with a gentle nudge to continue working.

- Require a daily submission of work.

- Allow students to go at their own pace.

- Use conditional releases to release work in chunks.

In terms of implications for research, our study was not designed to take into consideration teachers' perspectives on motivation in synchronous versus asynchronous contexts of high school DE. However, references to the importance of real-time interaction and communication, F2F meetings, time delays, and personal voice suggest that synchronicity may play an important role in motivation in DE at the high school level. This is a hypothesis that might be investigated in future studies. The study of motivation at this level might also be approached through research-validated frameworks such as the learner-centered principles, which include a motivational dimension. [R.M] Bernard et al. proposed using this framework for design and analysis of DE environments in order to "explor[e] the cognitive and motivational processes involved in learning at a distance." In addition, other analytical frameworks and theories specifically designed for DE environments which have been applied mostly to postsecondary settings, such as transactional distance theory and the community of inquiry model, might help provide new insights into motivation in high school DE.

| *"It's easy to miss just how much inflexibility is introduced into American life by the traditional public school approach, but those rigidities are legion."*

Consider Alternative Schooling: Column

Glenn Harlan Reynolds

Glenn Harlan Reynolds is a professor of law at the University of Tennessee and the author of The New School: How the Information Age Will Save American Education from Itself. *In the following viewpoint, he argues that public schools were originally designed to regiment students and prepare them for factory jobs. He says that this regimentation puts restrictions on American life, by, for example, forcing parents to live near good schools, even if they wouldn't live in those locations otherwise. Out of school, in online learning, he says, his daughter had more time to pursue interests and projects, without the time-wasting regimentation of public schools. He predicts that more and more students will move to online learning in the future.*

As you read, consider the following questions:

1. According to Reynolds, why did Horace Mann look to Prussia as a model for US public schools?

2. What restrictions does Reynolds say public school schedules put on families' time?

3. What projects was Reynolds's daughter able to pursue once she left public school?

Last week, I wrote here[1] about zero-tolerance stupidity, suggesting that as schools grow more and more willing to punish and stigmatize kids for reasons of bureaucratic convenience, it might be parental malpractice to put your kids in public schools. But there's another problem with public schools that goes beyond these kinds of problems: Even when they work well, public schools introduce all sorts of costs and rigidities into everyday life.

That's not surprising. Public schools were designed to be rigid. Back in the 19th century, when Massachusetts Board of Education Secretary Horace Mann[2] toured Europe looking for models of public education to import to America, the one he chose came from Prussia. Inflexibility and uniformity were Prussian specialties, and when Mann brought Prussian-style education to America, those characteristics were seen not as a bug but as a feature.

School was practice for working in the factory. Thus, the traditional public school: like a factory, it runs by the bell. Like machines in a factory, desks and students are lined up in orderly rows. When shifts (classes) change, the bell rings again, and students go on to the next class. And within each class, the subjects are the same, the assignments are the same, and the examinations are the same, regardless of the characteristics of individual students.

This had its advantages back during the Industrial Revolution[3], an assembly-line era where uniformity was more important than anything else, when Henry Ford[4] was happy to sell you a car in any color you wanted, so long as it was black[5]. But this is the 21st century, and now times have changed. You can buy a thousand different kinds of shampoo, so why should your kid have only one kind of education?

Many parents, thus, are embracing alternative education— like homeschooling[6] or online school[7]—not only as a way of escaping the often-poor instructional quality and questionable discipline of public schools, but also as a way of escaping the rigidities they bring.

It's easy to miss just how much inflexibility is introduced into American life by the traditional public school approach, but those rigidities are legion.

Real estate prices[8], for example, are heavily influenced by the quality of local public schools. Poor people often can't afford to attend top-flight public schools because they can't afford to live in the wealthy district. People who own property in those districts, meanwhile, stand to lose a significant amount of their home's value if the school board rezones them into a district with less-favored schools. Often people are forced to live in areas they'd otherwise rather not—because of long commutes, for example—simply in order to avail their kids of a decent education. By cutting the link between location and school quality, those problems could be eliminated, likely resulting in substantial savings for society— and parents.

And the intractability isn't just about space. It's also about time. Without a public school schedule, vacations can be taken when the family wants to, not when school bureaucrats schedule them; school days can be moved around to accommodate parents' work schedules and medical needs, and, perhaps most importantly, kids with more flexible school hours are more able to enter the workplace, which can be more educational than many things that happen in school.

US Median Home Sale Price vs. Elementary School Test Scores

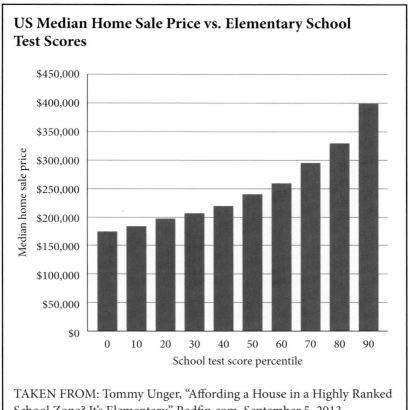

TAKEN FROM: Tommy Unger, "Affording a House in a Highly Ranked School Zone? It's Elementary," Redfin.com, September 5, 2013.

I can attest to this firsthand. My daughter did most of her high school online, after spending one day in ninth grade keeping track of how the public high school she attended spent her time. At the end of eight hours in school, she concluded, she had spent about 2½ hours on actual learning.

Switching to online school let her make sure that every hour counted. The flexibility also allowed her to work three days a week for a local TV-production company, where she got experience researching and writing for programs shown on the Biography Channel[9], A&E[10], etc., something she couldn't have done had she been nailed down in a traditional school. And she still managed to graduate a year early, at age 16, to head off to a "public Ivy" to study engineering. Did she miss out on socializing at school? Possibly, but at her job she got to spend more time with talented, hardworking adults, which may have been better. (And, as a friend pointed out, nobody ever got shot or pregnant at online school.)

Our experience with the flexibility offered by online schooling was a real eye-opener: You tend to take the restrictions imposed by the public school system for granted, as part of the background, until suddenly they're gone. I predict that over the next few years, a lot more eyes will open. Public schools will have to work hard if they are to keep up.

Notes

1. http://www.usatoday.com/story/opinion/2013/12/30/preschool-kids-education -grades-column/4239891/

2. http://books.google.com/books?id=xV2vZ4ESFPYC&pg=PA17&lpg=PA17&dq =Massachusetts+Board+of+Education+Secretary+Horace+Mann+prussia&source =bl&ots=WhGU4rpPVP&sig=ExTmmGJ7GMuRSCc-ilu7i7f-f68&hl=en&sa=X &ei=CJTJUvDRApK-kQerjoHACA&ved=0CGsQ6AEwCQ#v=onepage&q=Mass achusetts%20Board%20of%20Education%20Secretary%20Horace%20Mann%20 prussia&f=false

3. http://www.history.com/topics/industrial-revolution

4. http://www.history.com/topics/henry-ford

5. http://www.modelt.ca/background.html

6. http://www.huffingtonpost.com/2011/03/16/home-schooling-mainstream_n_836 591.html

7. http://www.huffingtonpost.com/2012/10/03/online-schools-face-backl_n_19351 25.html

8. http://blog.redfin.com/blog/2013/09/paying-more-for-a-house-with-a-top-public -school-its-elementary.html#.U9AOqLFa_5R

9. http://www.biography.com/

10. http://www.aetv.com/

> *"Colorado taxpayers will spend $100 million this year on online schools that are largely failing their elementary and high school students."*

Online K–12 Schools in Colorado Are Failing Students

Burt Hubbard and Nancy Mitchell

Burt Hubbard is the editorial director of Rocky Mountain PBS I-News; Nancy Mitchell is a longtime education reporter. In the following viewpoint, the authors discuss a study of online learning in Colorado. They conclude that many students who enter online learning do not remain with the program, and that the constant movement into and out of the program lowers test scores. They also report that the online schools siphon away public school funding. State money follows students; therefore, funding is taken away from public schools and given to the online schools when a student transfers. However, that money often does not go back to the public schools, even if the student drops out of the program.

As you read, consider the following questions:

1. According to the I-News/EdNews analysis, are the students who go into online courses at risk? What evidence shows this to be the case?

2. How did recruiters from GOAL attract students from St. Vrain Valley School District, according to the authors?

3. According to the viewpoint, how did Janette Lopez benefit from online education?

*I*n a 10-month investigation, the I-News Network and Education News Colorado examined the burgeoning business on online K–12 schools in Colorado. The findings:

Colorado taxpayers will spend $100 million this year [2011] on online schools that are largely failing their elementary and high school students, state education records and interviews with school officials show.

The money includes millions in tax dollars that are going to K–12 online schools for students who are no longer there.

The result: While online students fall further behind academically—their counterparts in the state's traditional public schools are suffering, too, because those schools must absorb former online students, while the virtual schools and their parent companies get to keep the state funding.

Online Schools Take Money Even When They Fail

Take the experience of high school senior Laura Johnson.

In the tiny Florence school district outside Pueblo, Johnson was one of 39 students who left Florence High School last year to sign up for online classes with GOAL Academy, one of the largest online charter schools in Colorado.

By January, she was back at Florence, disillusioned by the online experience and trying to make up for her lost time in class. She was joined by a dozen of her former online class-mates.

Those 39 students who left Florence High School for GOAL represented one of every 10 students in the school. When they left, so did nearly a quarter million dollars in state funding—the equivalent of four to five teachers' salaries. When a dozen of the students returned to Florence High midyear, the funding to educate them did not come with them. GOAL got to keep it.

The I-News Network, a Colorado-based in-depth news consortium, and one of its partners, the nonprofit Education News Colorado, spent 10 months investigating what's really happening with thousands of Colorado K–12 students who try an online school each year.

The investigation used previously unreleased Colorado Department of Education data to document the path of 10,500 students who were enrolled in the 10 largest online schools beginning in 2008. Those students accounted for more than 90 percent of all online students for the 2008–09 school year. The analysis found that in Colorado:

- Half the online students wind up leaving within a year. When they do, they're often further behind academi-cally than when they started.

- Online schools produce three times as many dropouts as they do graduates. One of every eight online stu-dents drops out of school permanently—a rate four times the state average.

- Millions of dollars are going to virtual schools for stu-dents who no longer attend online classes.

- The churn of students in and out of online schools is putting pressure on brick-and-mortar schools, which then must find money in their budgets to educate students who come from online schools midyear.

"We're bleeding money to a program that doesn't work," state senate president Brandon Shaffer, D-Longmont, said after being informed of the I-News/EdNews findings earlier this month. Last week, Shaffer asked the state audit committee for an emergency audit of online schools to be completed before the state legislature meets in January.

Shaffer, who is running for Congress, said the public should know about the findings, especially given the state's budget woes.

"We spend over $100 million a year on online schools now—in an environment where we're cutting $200 to $270 million a year from brick-and-mortar schools," Shaffer said.

Why Students Leave Online Schools

Officials with the online programs said a variety of factors contribute to the high rate of students leaving the programs.

Reasons for the turnover include working with an at-risk student population that sees online learning as their last resort, brief experimentation with a new learning process, and parents not being able to stay home to oversee their children's studies, said Heather O'Mara, executive director of Hope Online [Learning Academy], one of the state's largest online programs.

"We are all so different, we are serving different audiences and students are enrolling for very different reasons," O'Mara said. "At Hope, we particularly target kids who are at risk, who have not been academically successful, not only at their previous school, probably several schools before that."

However, the I-News/EdNews analysis of state data shows that most online school students do not appear to be at-risk students. Only about 120 students of the more than 10,000 entering online programs last year were identified as previous dropouts returning to school, and only 290 entered online schools after spending the prior year in an alternative school for troubled youth.

In addition, most are not struggling academically when they leave their traditional schools. Among the 2,400 online students who had taken a state standardized reading test in a brick-and-motor school the year before, the analysis showed that more than half had scored proficient or better.

The analysis also looked at dropouts—those students who leave school permanently. In Colorado's online schools, dropouts outnumber graduates by three to one. That's the reverse of the statewide average, where graduates outnumber dropouts by three to one.

Online Schools Are Booming

Online schools are thriving—in Colorado and nationally—using technology to educate students who need flexible scheduling or struggle in conventional classrooms. In Colorado, online schools grew seven times faster than conventional schools last year.

Students take classes, usually on computers provided by the online schools, and typically use e-mail or virtual chats to get teacher support. Some schools require a set amount of teacher contact, live or virtual; others do not.

Online schools may be created as district-run programs, or they can operate through charters or contracts with a school district or the state Charter School Institute. They can serve students in a single district or across the state.

Colorado's first online school opened in 1995, with 13 students—mostly from Denver and most on academic probation. It was headquartered in the San Luis Valley's Monte Vista School District.

Online schools were popular in small, rural districts, which typically get higher per-pupil funding. That changed in 2007 and online students are now funded at a flat rate of $6,228, slightly less than average per-pupil funding statewide.

Schools get that set amount of per-pupil funding based on student counts taken at the beginning of October each year. This year, Colorado expects to spend $100 million in state funds for some 18,000 students to attend online schools.

In each of the past three years, however, half the online students have left their schools within a year.

State documents make it difficult to pinpoint exactly when students leave a school. However, a comparison of the October student count data and districts' end-of-year data, shows the number of midyear transfers was at least 1,000 students a year—and perhaps many more. That means at least $6 million annually went to online schools for students who weren't there.

Of 10,500 students in the largest online programs in fall 2008, more than half—or 5,600—left their virtual schools by the fall of 2009. They were more than replaced by 7,400 new recruits by that fall. That new group also experienced high turnover, with more than a third of the students leaving by the end of that school year, the analysis showed.

By October 2010, only about a quarter of the students remained in their same online program after two years.

The student turnover in the programs concerns state educators and lawmakers who fear profit and overzealous student recruitment are taking precedence over educating students.

"There isn't much effort put into keeping those kids in that school," Shaffer, the state senate president, said. "It's all about boosting their numbers for the count date, then forget about the kids."

Randy DeHoff, who spent 12 years on the State Board of Education before becoming GOAL Academy's director of strategic planning last November, said online schools need to help students determine who is likely to succeed in an online learning environment.

"One of the things the online schools need to do a better job of in that recruitment and enrollment phase is trying to give a student a real clear idea of what an online program's about (and) what their responsibilities are," DeHoff said.

Diana Sirko, deputy commissioner of education in Colorado, said she intends to put together a task force to look at the problems created by skyrocketing online enrollment, especially the high turnover. It could lead the state to ask for legislative changes, she said.

"I think it's problematic for the student . . . we know that mobility contributes to a lack of success for students," Sirko said. "What we hear from some of the school districts who receive children halfway through the year who've started in online is there may have been a two- or three-month gap as they left one and began the next."

Dropping Scores

The I-News/EdNews analysis looked at test scores for online students who'd previously been in traditional brick-and-mortar schools, and found that scores dropped once students entered online schools. For example, 59 percent had scored proficient or above in reading while in a brick-and-motor school. But after a year in online school, only 51 percent achieved that score.

Top officials at some school districts said they have seen firsthand how the turnover has hurt their students and their finances.

The St. Vrain [Valley] School District in Longmont lost 70 students to GOAL last year after heavy recruiting by the online program. St. Vrain superintendent Don Haddad said GOAL recruiters driving around in recreational vehicles emblazoned with GOAL's logos made pitches to high school students during their school lunch hours. GOAL also has storefront operations in many malls along the Front Range.

DeHoff, the former state education board member now at GOAL, said the emphasis on recruiting stems from an effort to reach students not being served by traditional schools. GOAL targets at-risk students.

"We're not trying to steal kids from districts, we're there serving the kids that districts either can't or don't want to serve," DeHoff said.

Many of GOAL's recruited students returned to St. Vrain schools in the middle of the year, behind in school, Haddad said. For many of the returning students, their time in the on-line program was "wasted," he said.

"These institutions, what they do is borderline unethical behavior in my mind," said Haddad, who supports online learning as a tool. "It's a moneymaking proposition and they have no problem sending the kids back after the October count. The sales job they get up front, it's a travesty."

Ken Crowell, executive director of GOAL Academy, strongly disagreed with Haddad's assessment.

"Those are really tough words coming from the superintendent," Crowell said. "I think he is definitely mistaken. That's unfortunate."

Haddad said the district lost more than $400,000 in state funding last year to GOAL's recruitment of students.

Florence High School principal Steve Wolfe said one in every 10 students at his school left for GOAL online last year after a summer recruiting blitz by a popular former Florence teacher hired by GOAL after his contract was not renewed. The GOAL recruitment included barbecues in the town park for prospective students, Wolfe said.

About a dozen of the students came back after Oct. 1, the official state count day to determine per-pupil funding. GOAL got the funding; Florence got the students back. Then the school had to find ways to help them catch up.

Laura Johnson, one of the returning students, said she signed up for GOAL in July after her former science teacher promised free college classes. But she was back at Florence High School by January with no credits earned.

Wasted Time

"I feel like I wasted an entire semester of my life," said Johnson, now working overtime to boost her grades in hopes the gap in her transcript will be less noticeable to colleges.

She said technology problems kept her from starting classes until September and the social isolation quickly convinced her that online was not a good fit.

"I don't think it's healthy for someone to stare at a computer screen for five hours straight," she said. "I think the most difficult part about it was trying to keep yourself on it."

However, for other students, the online programs are a boon.

Janette Lopez, 19, is a teen mom who said she dropped out of Pueblo schools because of child care issues.

Lopez enrolled in the GOAL online program, which assigns students to teachers based on their geographic area. It has opened 13 "drop-in centers" statewide where students and teachers can meet.

The model has worked for Lopez, whose son is now 4. Lopez was assigned a teacher who came to her home and who fit classes around a second pregnancy.

"I really wanted my education and I just went for it," said Lopez, who plans to graduate in December and attend community college. "She was right there with me."

Some superintendents bristle over the fact that some online programs are sponsored by other school districts that typically receive a portion of their per-pupil funding.

For example, Hope Online is sponsored by the Douglas County School District, but few of the district's students use the Hope program, the analysis found. Hope pays Douglas County about $2 million a year for support services such as professional development and special education.

That irks Randy Miller, superintendent of the Eaton School District in Weld County. His district lost a battle to keep a Hope online school out with the argument it wasn't needed.

"How does Douglas County know more about what is needed in Eaton than our own board?" Miller said.

Amy Anderson was recently named to oversee innovation and choice, including online schools, for the Colorado Department of Education. She said she understands the usefulness of online programs for students such as Lopez, but worries about the turnover.

"There are other schools that are just churning kids and I don't feel that is good for kids," Anderson said. "So how can we prevent that? Those are the challenges that the authorizers of online charters are starting to talk about."

In the meantime, some Colorado school districts—including both Florence and St. Vrain—have chosen their own way to combat losses to the online schools: They're starting their own online programs.

> "*The advantages of a MOOC for K–12 education are clear enough, though. Schools could use them to bridge the teacher shortage, particularly in math and science.*"

MOOC: Will These Four Letters Change K–12?

Michelle Locke

Michelle Locke is a contributing writer for Scholastic Administrator. *In the following viewpoint, she discusses MOOCs, massive open online courses, which are growing more popular in higher education. Locke says that MOOCs, which are generally free and open to all, could have many advantages for K–12 education, supplementing teacher shortages and offering students the opportunity to take specialized courses. She notes that there are problems with MOOCs as well, including high dropout rates and difficulty in preventing cheating. However, she concludes that MOOCs may start to be a more important part of K–12 education.*

As you read, consider the following questions:

1. According to Locke, how do MOOCs differ from online courses already used in high schools?

2. Why does Jennifer Whiting believe that MOOCs are not likely to benefit most high school students?

3. According to MOOC provider Coursera, how do high school students use its services?

Cheap, hip, and tailored for the YouTube generation, MOOCs—massive open online courses—are the hottest thing in higher ed right now. But do they have potential for K–12 instruction?

Absolutely, says Raymond Schroeder, director of the Center for Online Learning, Research and Service at the University of Illinois at Springfield. There's already talk of using the MOOC model to offer more advanced-placement high school courses, and it's likely interest will continue to grow. Many trends, online learning among them, begin in higher education and then move to the K–12 level, says Schroeder. "I think there's potential for MOOCs to penetrate deep into K–12."

In the realm of higher ed, accredited online learning has been around for a while. MOOCs are a slightly different breed. They're usually free and do not confer class credit, although some companies are teaming with universities to provide proctored exams so students can gain credits from them. Stylistically, MOOCs borrow from the youth-centric worlds of online gaming and social media. Information is delivered in chunks—snappy, 15-minute presentations, with pauses for students to take quizzes (and receive instant feedback). And—this is the massive part—enrollment is essentially open to anyone who can get online, which means class size can grow into the tens of thousands.

Online classes that size require a high degree of student motivation, and they vary greatly in approach. Some are free-wheeling exercises in personal enrichment; others come with structured study groups and proctored exams; and a few offer credit in partnership with a brick-and-mortar university. Generally, MOOCs have high dropout rates, not a workable option for K–12, and weeding out cheaters is a challenge. (Schroeder points out that the low completion rate—which has been estimated at 10 percent—is misleading, since signing up for a MOOC now is basically commitment free, something that wouldn't be true for high school students.)

The advantages of a MOOC for K–12 education are clear enough, though. Schools could use them to bridge the teacher shortage, particularly in math and science. A high school struggling to find a teacher qualified to lead 20 students in AP calculus could tap into the expertise of a top-flight university professor. And schools with just a handful of students ready for calculus could plug them into a MOOC as well.

Robin Worley, who is working on a distance-learning project for Kamehameha Schools, a private college-prep school in Hawaii, thinks MOOCs' potential for K–12 education outweighs the drawbacks. She has started the website k12mooc.org to build a community of like-minded educators. Response so far has come from parents, administrators, and teachers, including one interested in creating a Spanish MOOC.

Imagining K–12 MOOCs

There would need to be changes for MOOCs to work in secondary and primary schools, says Worley. She envisions subject experts creating a K–12 course with top-of-the-line content that thousands of students—across the country and beyond—can access. "Being able to utilize teachers who are experts in their area would be a huge benefit," she says.

Students would watch content together (sharing a computer if resources are scant). A facilitator would lead classroom discussions and supervise group work. And with age-appropriate content, the blended-learning approach could work at all grade levels, says Worley.

Schroeder thinks MOOCs are going to start catching on as more high school students start taking them on their own (as they no doubt already are—"adult" and higher-ed MOOCs have no age restrictions). He, too, thinks that they'll ultimately be used in conjunction with a teacher in the discipline on hand to "occasionally hover over the student and, at the very least, be there."

Just One More Potential Tool

Others have reservations about using MOOCs as part of K–12 schooling.

NEA senior policy analyst Mike Kaspar says MOOCs have merit as an enrichment tool, but he remains wary. "Just because it's great technology and higher ed has been doing it doesn't necessarily mean it would transition well" to high school or below, says Kaspar.

The problem with MOOCs, he says, is that they can't provide teacher-student interaction. "It looks like it's the silver bullet; it looks like it will take care of the teacher shortage issue, but it doesn't," he says. "It doesn't provide for the education that the student needs."

Jennifer Whiting, of the all-online Florida Virtual School (FLVS), also sees MOOCs as a supplement rather than a major instructional component at the K–12 level. As a leading provider of online education—free to Florida residents and available for a fee in other states—FLVS has learned that it takes a "caring, interactive teacher" to make a successful student, Whiting says. "That teacher forms a relationship with the student that I don't think we're going to get in MOOCs." Even an excellent instructor can't provide that in a class with hundreds of students. Meanwhile, FLVS has discovered that "it takes a team" to deter cheating. "When you've got a massive student load, it's hard to know when cheating is happening. Nobody's going to be able to really tell if your five hundredth student is copying from the thousandth student."

However, Whiting does expect the K–12 community to start using MOOCs as supplements—for instance, having students take part in an SAT prep MOOC.

MOOCs Are Expanding Learning

One of the recent developments of distance education programs is known as MOOCs [massive open online courses]. Starting with a small number of students in North American universities, free and open online courses are currently being offered by Coursera through some of the world's best-known universities. Universities such as Stanford University, the University of Melbourne and the University of Queensland are some current examples of universities that offer MOOCs. Despite the challenges and concerns about the quality of education in MOOCs, this mode of distance learning has become a reality for many universities in the world. What is fascinating about the MOOC development is that anyone with the technology available to them can undertake a course at university level in an open and "unfiltered" way, without regard to entrance requirements and prior knowledge or learning. This is a major step beyond the original open university ideas developed in the 20th century in the United Kingdom. Whether the MOOC development (which has attracted hundreds of thousands of students in a very short time) will lead to formal qualifications and challenge the exclusive university market is yet to be seen but is a concern for many in the higher education sector.

Len Cairns and Khalid Alshahrani,
"Online Learning: Models and Impact in the 21st Century,"
in Teaching and Learning Online: New Models of Learning
for a Connected World. Vol. 2. Eds. Brian Sutton
and Anthony Basiel. New York: Routledge, 2013.

Where Will It Lead?

Coursera, a major MOOC provider, has no current plans to create classes for K–12 students, according to cofounder Andrew Ng. "We are aware that many students at the high school level have been taking courses on Coursera to prepare for college or to gain extra knowledge in topics of interest," he says. "We do not view MOOCs as a full replacement for traditional education; however, we believe that traditional learning approaches can be improved by implementing education technologies such as online learning to promote better learning outcomes and meet the needs of students at various levels."

Even though there's a lot of excitement in higher ed about MOOCs, universities are still figuring out how to use them and there are concerns over the impact they could have on the value of a degree. Schools are well aware that MOOCs have the potential to generate real money—imagine 50,000 students signing up at $10 a head. And schools can use MOOCs to broaden course offerings at no cost and free up staff. Coursera, launched in April 2012 by Ng and fellow Stanford professor Daphne Koller, has partnerships with more than 60 universities, and the American Council on Education recently recommended credit for five of Coursera's courses.

With funding for education shrinking, Schroeder expects to see more attention paid to MOOCs and more experimentation with different models. The Center for Online Learning, Research and Service is studying the effectiveness of MOOC teaching methods, part of the wide-ranging American Council on Education research study on whether MOOCs are worthy of college credit. Eventually, the study will track university students to see how those who used MOOCs did compared with those who took conventional courses.

"We see all these possibilities, and there are people who are already finding success," says Schroeder, "but we're very early in the process of identifying what's the best model and how we can optimize this for the student."

Whatever its future in the K–12 classroom may be, says Whiting, "people are starting to wake up and take notice."

> *"A closer inspection—one that moves beyond the mania and scrutinizes the details—suggests that MOOCs may be falling short of many of their promises."*

Massive Open Online Courses Are Overhyped and Have Serious Problems for K–12

Audrey Watters

Audrey Watters is a journalist who has written about education technology for MindShift, Inside Higher Ed, *Edutopia, and her own blog,* Hack Education. *In the following viewpoint, she says that many people hope that MOOCs—massive open online courses—can lower the cost of education and bring learning to students cheaply and efficiently, whether in college or K–12. Watters, argues, though, that MOOC graduation rates are extremely low. She also says that the little that is known about who enrolls in MOOCs suggests that the courses are not reaching underserved populations. She concludes that MOOCs are overhyped and that schools at both the college and high school level should be cautious about embracing them.*

As you read, consider the following questions:

1. According to Watters, when did the hype about MOOCs begin?

2. Why aren't demographic data available for many MOOCs?

3. When people say that MOOCs can change and improve rapidly, what is the unspoken implication, according to Watters?

In the fall of 2011, Stanford University offered three of its engineering courses—Artificial Intelligence [AI], Machine Learning, and Introduction to Databases—for free online. Anyone with Internet access could sign up for them. As Sebastian Thrun, the director of Stanford's Artificial Intelligence Laboratory, tells the story, he assumed just a handful of people would enroll in his graduate-level AI class. Instead, more than 160,000 students registered. A massive number.

That's when the enormous hype began about massive open online courses, better known as "MOOCs." Since then, Thrun and his fellow lab professors Daphne Koller and Andrew Ng have founded education organizations that offer free online classes. Thrun's start-up is called Udacity (in part, a takeoff on the word "audacious"), and Koller and Ng's is Coursera. In December 2011, in response to Stanford's initiatives, MIT [Massachusetts Institute of Technology] launched its own effort, called MITX (short for "Massachusetts Innovation & Technology Exchange"), and a few months later joined forces with Harvard, drolly changing the name of the organization to EdX. A consortium of British universities has also created its own MOOC platform, FutureLearn. So far, more than 90 universities worldwide have teamed up with one or more of these MOOC providers, prompting the *New York Times* to crown 2012 as "The Year of the MOOC."

Although it's clear that there's a flurry of interest in MOOCs among universities, higher-ed students, the tech industry, and pundits, these free online courses are also likely to have a significant impact on K–12 librarians and other educators. As Joyce Valenza, a teacher librarian at Springfield Township High School in Pennsylvania, pointed out on her *SLJ* blog *Never Ending Search*, MOOCs "can reach tens of thousands of students of all ages, regardless of geography or social class. They have the potential to be equalizers. MOOCs have the potential to disrupt traditional education platforms. And experts predict they will."

In fact, according to *Education Week*, MOOCs are already making waves among the school-yard set: the University of Miami Global Academy (UMGA), a private online school for middle and high schoolers, is already exploring how to use MOOCs to serve its 143 students. Late last year [2012], UMGA "launched what may be the first free MOOC for high school students—a three-week test prep class designed to get students ready for the College Board's SAT subject test in biology," reports Valenza.

The Price of Popularity

No doubt, the excitement over MOOCs stems from many of the thorny issues facing education today, including the argument that school curriculums don't provide students with the knowledge and skills that they need to be successful. But the most powerful case for MOOCs' rising popularity reflects the soaring cost of college tuition and the accompanying increase in student loan debt. By some estimates, the cost of obtaining a college degree has grown almost twelvefold over the last few decades, and in 2012, our nation's student loan debt hit a record high, surpassing the $1 trillion mark—a figure larger than the country's outstanding credit card debt.

Still, the allure of a cost-free education is only part of MOOCs' appeal. Their open enrollment means that anyone—no matter their age, level of educational attainment, or geography—can (at least in theory) participate. And both the "massive" and the "online" components of these courses mean that they can handle the incredible and ever-growing global demand for higher education. According to UNESCO [United Nations Educational, Scientific and Cultural Organization], within the next decade this demand will reach more than 200 million students a year, most of whom will come from developing countries. To meet that demand in a traditional way would require building thousands of new college campuses. The alternative? Simply take advantage of Internet technologies—something that MOOCs aim to do.

By framing the future of education like this—on campus or on the Internet, off-line versus online—MOOCs have sparked much talk about "the end of the university as we know it." *New York Times* columnist Thomas Friedman has described MOOCs as a "revolution," and Stanford University president John Hennessy sees online education as a "tsunami coming." Thrun himself believes that as a result of MOOCs, in 50 years there'll be only 10 universities left on the entire planet.

Is this rhetoric or reality? It remains to be seen. But as MOOC mania continues to grow, accompanied by the belief that these courses will ultimately shape our schools' future, it's worth pausing to look more closely at what these massive online classes offer. Although tens of thousands of students register for MOOCs, relatively few actually complete the courses. For instance, roughly 14 percent of those who enrolled in Thrun's 2011 AI course passed the class. And that figure is quite a bit higher than the average completion rate for MOOCs, which according to graduate student Katy Jordan's research at Open University hovers at around 7.6 percent.

Take EdX's circuits and electronics class. More than 150,000 people signed up for it, but only 7,157—a measly five percent—completed the class. And just 69,221 registrants looked at the first problem set and a scant 13,569 took the midterm. Of the 10,262 students who showed up for the final exam, 5,800 people received a passing score.

Why is the attrition rate so high? And why does this pattern persist in most MOOCs? Which students are succeeding and which are failing? Despite a lot of speculation (ranging from students simply being too busy with other pursuits to the courses themselves being too hard or too easy), not much is known.

Part of the problem stems from the registration process for many of these MOOCs—just enter an e-mail address and you're in. As such, there aren't a lot of demographic details about the students who are taking the classes. No questions are asked during the sign-up process about age, gender, race or ethnicity, location, educational background. These questions are sometimes asked in surveys (voluntarily completed), but the demographics of MOOC students aren't routinely gathered. As it stands, much of what we do know comes from professors releasing their own data, rather than from any of the MOOC service providers themselves.

Georgia Tech's Tucker Balch, an associate professor at the School of Interactive Computing, released the following information based on the survey of students who took part in his recent Coursera class, "Computational Investing." Of the 2,535 students who completed the course (or 4.8 percent of those enrolled), 34 percent were from the United States and 27 percent came from non-OECD [Organisation for Economic Co-operation and Development] countries. The average age of participants was 35 (ranging from 17 to 74). Seventy percent were white. Ninety-two percent were male. And more than 50 percent of the students already had a master's degree or a PhD. Clearly, this is hardly the "typical" undergraduate population (although it's worth noting that "Computational Investing" isn't really a "typical" or introductory class). Nonetheless, these figures do raise questions about who exactly is being served by today's MOOCs: Is it "learners" from around the world? Or, for lack of a better word, is it "knowers" from the U.S.?

Behind the Hype

Much of the hoopla surrounding MOOCs is that they increase access to higher education and liberate students (and professors and institutions) from the tyranny of a large lecture class. But a closer inspection—one that moves beyond the mania and scrutinizes the details—suggests that MOOCs may be falling short of many of their promises.

Most of Coursera's and Udacity's MOOCs still rely almost entirely on lectures—they're just videotaped and delivered online, and occasionally divided into smaller, 5- to 20-minute chunks. It's possible that the reliance on lectures—and by extension on the automatically graded multiple-choice quizzes scattered intermittently between the courses' videos—reflects these MOOCs' origins in the science and engineering departments. But it's clear that this teaching format (on- or off-line) doesn't really work for many academic disciplines or for many types of college courses, particularly for students more accustomed to active classrooms, hands-on experimentation, and student-professor discussions.

But "it's early" insist proponents of MOOCs, as they emphasize the experimental nature of these courses and their ability to iterate rapidly. (The often-unspoken implication here is that traditional universities and their professors are inflexible and unchanging.) Despite the unanswered questions about who precisely these classes are serving, more and more universities are hopping on the MOOC bandwagon, seemingly because many fear, as former Princeton University president William Bowen recently quipped in a *New York Times* article that they might otherwise be "left behind." And this impulse, almost more than any of the other arguments about access or cost, seems to be driving much of the narrative surrounding why MOOCs, why now.

Interestingly, many of these narratives about the history, structure, and rationale of MOOCs overlook the origins of massive open online courses. The term doesn't come from the courses offered by Stanford AI professors in 2011, but rather it was coined in association with an open online course—"Connectivism and Connective Knowledge"—offered in 2008 by the University of Manitoba. This class—and the connectivist MOOCs like it that are still offered today—looked quite different from the lecture-based, learning-management, system-focused courses that Udacity, Coursera, EdX, and the like offer. Students could take part by using the technologies of their choice—blogs, YouTube videos, synchronous video discussions, and so on—and this participation was aggregated via links and RSS feeds into a main site, one that was openly available on the Web.

But it wasn't just the tools that were different; the academic backgrounds of the professors behind these innovations were different, too. They were largely from the field of education rather than computer science, and the emphasis was on building learning networks and communities—and helping learners think about how to negotiate online learning spaces—and not simply on replicating or scaling the content delivery of typical engineering courses.

It's interesting that this origin of MOOCs remains largely ignored (and unfortunate as there are decades of experience from those who've taught online and taught with technology that are being left out of many of these discussions), but it's not particularly surprising. MOOC mania taps into powerful narratives—both true and false—about the relevancy of the curriculum, the cost of college, and the adaptability of education institutions. Many institutions are joining MOOCs, hoping that the mania pans out and that these free online classes will, if nothing else, keep their brands up-to-date. But the questions about who exactly they're serving with these classes will have to be answered sooner or later as having tens of thousands of students sign up for a class is hardly the right metric upon which to build the future of education.

As K–12 schools begin to investigate MOOCs—weighing their potential benefits and challenges—it will be crucial to ask questions about course completion and student success. While these online classes might offer a way to deliver online education to the masses, it will be just as important—if not more so—to think through how we can provide massive student support.

Periodical and Internet Sources Bibliography

The following articles have been selected to supplement the diverse views presented in this chapter.

Michelle R. Davis	"MOOC Targets Needs of K–12 Teachers, Students," *Education Week*, October 23, 2013.
Susan Edelman	"'Fail Factory' Teacher Churns Through 475 Students per Year," *New York Post*, February 9, 2014.
Lisa Fleisher	"High School with No Walls Takes Shape: Proposed iZone Academy Could Open Next Year," *Wall Street Journal*, December 10, 2013.
Andy Ford	"Florida Education Association President Andy Ford: Digital Education Can Be Valuable If Correctly Used," *Orlando Sentinel*, April 5, 2012.
Trip Gabriel	"More Pupils Are Learning Online, Fueling Debate on Quality," *New York Times*, April 5, 2011.
Tamar Lewin	"After Setbacks, Online Courses Are Rethought," *New York Times*, December 10, 2013.
Mary Beth Marklein	"Online-Education Trend Expands," *USA Today*, November 19, 2012.
Nick Pandolfo	"The Teacher You've Never Met: Inside an Online High School Class," *Time*, June 13, 2012.
Kelsey Sheehy	"States, Districts Require Online Ed for High School Graduation," *U.S. News & World Report*, October 24, 2012.
Patrick Welsh	"Column: High Schools, Take the Online Course," *USA Today*, January 8, 2013.

For Further Discussion

Chapter 1

1. Heather Vogell reports that the Hall County School District forced underachieving students to transfer to an alternative school to help lower the district's dropout rates. Do you think this was the right course of action for the school district to take? Explain your reasoning.

2. Nirvi Shah argues that students with mental disabilities thrive when they are placed in mainstream classes instead of special education classes. What do you see as some of the advantages and disadvantages of including students with mental disabilities in mainstream classrooms? What do you see as some of the advantages and disadvantages of placing such students in special education classes?

3. As Barbara Jones points out, the parents of special education students in a Los Angeles school district are protesting the transfer of their children from special education centers to traditional schools. Do you believe these parents have the right to choose the school their children should attend? Provide reasons to support your answer.

Chapter 2

1. Richard Fry claims that foreign-born Hispanics with a GED earn more money than foreign-born workers with a high school diploma. What are some reasons for this? Do you think this wage difference is justified? Explain your reasoning.

2. After reading the viewpoints by Kavitha Cardoza and James E. Causey, do you think the new GED test being released in 2014 will benefit or burden test takers? Cite evidence from the viewpoints to support your answer.

Chapter 3

1. Kevin Booker and his colleagues argue that charter schools offer students a good opportunity to graduate high school and attend college. In your opinion, should students attend charter schools instead of traditional schools? What evidence from the viewpoint led you to your answer? Explain your reasoning.

2. Jackie Hardy contends that charter schools help close the achievement gap, particularly among minority students. Do you agree or disagree with Hardy? Explain your reasoning.

3. Genevieve Siegel-Hawley and Erica Frankenberg point to studies that show that magnet schools are more racially diverse and have better academic outcomes than traditional schools. After reading the viewpoint, do you think there is a link between the diversity offered in magnet schools and the schools' high academic achievement? Cite evidence from the viewpoint to support your answer.

Chapter 4

1. According to Glenn Harlan Reynolds, online schools offer more flexibility and freedom than public schools, which were, as Reynolds argues, originally designed to prepare students for factory jobs. How does the flexibility of online learning compare to the regimentation of public schools? Can this be beneficial to students? Explain, citing examples from the viewpoint.

2. Michelle Locke contends that although massive open online courses (MOOCs) could benefit K–12 education, these courses have some drawbacks. What are the drawbacks that Locke cites? In your opinion, what are some additional benefits and drawbacks offered by MOOCs that Locke does not mention?

Organizations to Contact

The editors have compiled the following list of organizations concerned with the issues debated in this book. The descriptions are derived from materials provided by the organizations. All have publications or information available for interested readers. The list was compiled on the date of publication of the present volume; the information provided here may change. Be aware that many organizations take several weeks or longer to respond to inquiries, so allow as much time as possible.

Achieve
1400 Sixteenth Street NW, Suite 510, Washington, DC   20036
(202) 419-1540 • fax: (202) 828-0911
website: www.achieve.org

Achieve is an independent, nonpartisan organization concerned with passing effective and meaningful education reform, such as raising academic standards and strengthening accountability. In 2005 it launched the American Diploma Project Network, which brings together business executives, school officials, and politicians to align high school standards and assessment and accountability systems. Achieve conducts extensive research and publishes state and national reports in addition to policy briefs. It also publishes a monthly e-newsletter, *Perspective*, which focuses on current issues and provides updates on recent initiatives.

Center for Education Reform (CER)
910 Seventeenth Street NW, 11th Floor
Washington, DC   20006
(800) 521-2118
website: www.edreform.com

The Center for Education Reform (CER) is a national organization dedicated to implementing effective educational reform. The CER website posts the latest research and press releases from the organization's experts; provides a forum for teachers, policy makers, and parents to discuss education issues; and offers a way for interested citizens to become involved in grassroots educational reform advocacy in their area. The CER's Media Bullpen is a virtual newsroom that offers online access to hundreds of education news stories daily, while its editorial staff reacts and responds to these stories in real time to engage and promote discussion of education topics.

Center for Public Education (CPE)
1680 Duke Street, Alexandria, VA   22314
(703) 838-6722 • fax: (703) 548-5613
e-mail: centerforpubliced@nsba.org
website: www.centerforpubliceducation.org

The Center for Public Education (CPE) is a resource center set up by the National School Boards Association (NSBA). CPE works to provide up-to-date information about public education in an effort to establish more public understanding about America's schools, more community-wide involvement, and better decision making by school leaders on behalf of all students in their classrooms. Among the many articles available at CPE's website are "Charter Schools: Finding Out the Facts: At a Glance" and "Keeping Kids in School: What Research Tells Us About Preventing Dropouts."

Center for Research on Education Outcomes (CREDO)
434 Galvez Mall, Stanford, CA   94305-6010
(650) 725-3431 • fax: (650) 723-1687
e-mail: credoatstanford@gmail.com
website: http://credo.stanford.edu

The Center for Research on Education Outcomes (CREDO) is a research center and think tank associated with Stanford University that focuses on compiling data on educational reform and student performance. CREDO works to provide innovative and effective educational reform policies and programs to improve the quality of American education. Some of CREDO's publications include "National Charter School Study 2013" and "Paying for A's: An Early Exploration of Student Rewards and Incentive Programs in Charter Schools."

George Lucas Educational Foundation
PO Box 3494, San Rafael, CA   94912-3494
(415) 662-1673
e-mail: info@edutopia.org
website: www.edutopia.org

The goal of the George Lucas Educational Foundation is to improve education through creative, evidence-based strategies that help children become lifelong learners. One way in which the foundation carries out its mission is through the Edutopia website. Edutopia works to spread the word about ideal, interactive learning environments and enable others to adapt these successes locally. One initiative on the website, Schools That Work, profiles schools around the country that are making innovative improvements to the way students learn. How-to videos and tips are provided to help other schools emulate the success. Edutopia produces classroom guides and videos, which are available online.

International Association for
K–12 Online Learning (iNACOL)
1934 Old Gallows Road, Suite 350, Vienna, VA   22182-4050
(888) 956-2265 • fax: (703) 752-6201
website: www.inacol.org

The International Association for K–12 Online Learning (iNACOL) is a nonprofit organization that advocates for increased access to quality online education programs. It facilitates the evaluation and dissemination of online learning programs, develops standards, and lobbies for policies that increase access and improve quality. The organization also assists in funding efforts for various online programs and provides a forum for administrators and participants to exchange ideas about how to improve and maintain the quality of virtual education. The iNACOL website links to a number of relevant reports and research publications and hosts a forum that posts the latest news in the industry.

National Alliance for Public Charter Schools

1101 Fifteenth Street NW, Suite 1010, Washington, DC   20005
(202) 289-2700 • fax: (202) 289-4009
e-mail: info@publiccharters.org
website: www.publiccharters.org

The National Alliance for Public Charter Schools is a nonprofit organization that works to support the spread of charter schools across the country, particularly in areas that could benefit from school choice. The organization advocates for charter school students, parents, teachers, and administrators with policy makers and politicians with the goal of passing legislation beneficial to the charter school movement and creating policies that will increase access to charter schools. One of the organization's aims is to eliminate "charter caps" that limit the number of charter schools in certain areas. The group's website provides fact sheets, reports and research, and a multimedia library that includes photos, videos, and audio recordings of recent events, speeches, and presentations.

National Alternative Education Association (NAEA)

10536 Knollwood Drive, Manassas, VA   20111
website: www.the-naea.org

Established in 2002, the National Alternative Education Association (NAEA) is a volunteer organization that provides advocacy and support for professionals who are involved with alternative education services. NAEA works to maintain effective guidelines for best practices and provides professional learning experiences to educators in the field. NAEA's website offers several publications, including "Exemplary Practices in Alternative Education: Indicators of Quality Programming" and "Promoting High Quality Alternative Education."

National Education Association (NEA)
1201 Sixteenth Street NW, Washington, DC   20036-3290
(202) 833-4000 • fax: (202) 822-7974
website: www.nea.org

Founded in 1857, the National Education Association (NEA) is an educator membership organization that works to advance the rights of educators and children. NEA focuses its energy on improving the quality of teaching, increasing student achievement, and making schools safe places to learn. NEA Today is a website that offers the latest stories on education topics as well as access to the *NEA Today* magazine. NEA also publishes *Thought & Action*, a journal focused on education theory; *Tomorrow's Teachers*, a resource for teachers; and *Higher Education Advocate*, a bimonthly newsletter that explores issues important in higher education.

US Department of Education
400 Maryland Avenue SW, Washington, DC   20202
(800) 872-5327
website: www.ed.gov

The US Department of Education is the federal department that establishes federal school funding policies, distributes funds, monitors school performance, and enforces federal law on discrimination. It also distributes financial aid to eligible students and oversees research on America's schools to determine the success of educational programs across the country. Publications available on the department's website include handbooks, research papers, speeches, congressional testimony, and in-depth studies on reform and funding topics. It also publishes a number of journals and newsletters, including *ED Review* and *Education Research News*.

Bibliography of Books

David C. Berliner and Gene V. Glass — *50 Myths and Lies That Threaten America's Public Schools: The Real Crisis in Education.* New York: Teachers College Press, 2014.

Joe Bower and P.L. Thomas, eds. — *De-Testing and De-Grading Schools: Authentic Alternatives to Accountability and Standardization.* New York: Peter Lang Publishing, 2013.

Jack Buckley and Mark Schneider — *Charter Schools: Hope or Hype?* Princeton, NJ: Princeton University Press, 2009.

Cathy Cavanaugh and Robert Blomeyer, eds. — *What Works in K–12 Online Learning.* Washington, DC: International Society for Technology in Education, 2007.

Cameron Curry — *Charter School Leadership: Elements for School Success.* Lanham, MD: Rowman & Littlefield, 2013.

Peter Demerath — *Producing Success: The Culture of Personal Advancement in an American High School.* Chicago, IL: University of Chicago Press, 2009.

Mark Drolsbaugh — *Madness in the Mainstream.* Spring House, PA: Handwave Publications, 2013.

Robin J. Lake, ed. *Unique Schools Serving Unique Students: Charter Schools and Children with Special Needs*. Seattle, WA: Center on Reinventing Public Education, 2010.

Kathleen Lynne Lane, Holly Mariah Menzies, Allison L. Bruhn, and Mary Crnobori *Managing Challenging Behaviors in Schools: Research-Based Strategies That Work*. New York: Guilford Press, 2011.

Christopher A. Lubienski and Peter C. Weitzel, eds. *The Charter School Experiment: Expectations, Evidence, and Implications*. Cambridge, MA: Harvard Education Press, 2010.

Gina A. Oliva and Linda Risser Lytle *Turning the Tide: Making Life Better for Deaf and Hard of Hearing Schoolchildren*. Washington, DC: Gallaudet University Press, 2014.

Ron Packard *Education Transformation: How K–12 Online Learning Is Bringing the Greatest Change to Education in 100 Years*. New York: Simon & Schuster, 2013.

Diane Ravitch *The Death and Life of the Great American School System: How Testing and Choice Are Undermining Education*. New York: Basic Books, 2011.

Diane Ravitch   *Reign of Error: The Hoax of the Privatization Movement and the Danger to America's Public Schools.* New York: Alfred A. Knopf, 2013.

Glenn Harlan Reynolds   *The New School: How the Information Age Will Save American Education from Itself.* New York: Encounter Books, 2014.

Russell W. Rumberger   *Dropping Out: Why Students Drop Out of High School and What Can Be Done About It.* Cambridge, MA: Harvard University Press, 2011.

Phil Smith, ed.   *Whatever Happened to Inclusion?: The Place of Students with Intellectual Disabilities in Education.* New York: Peter Lang, 2010.

Elliot Washor and Charles Mojkowski   *Leaving to Learn: How Out-of-School Learning Increases Student Engagement and Reduces Dropout Rates.* Portsmouth, NH: Heinemann, 2013.

Jeannette Webb   *Homeschooling to Open Doors: Smart High School Choices for Great College Options.* Custer City, OK: Prairie Song Publishing, 2013.

Richard Whitmire   *On the Rocketship: How Top Charter Schools Are Pushing the Envelope.* San Francisco, CA: Jossey-Bass, 2014.

Jeffrey R. Young   *Beyond the MOOC Hype: A Guide to Higher Education's High-Tech Disruption*. Washington, DC: Chronicle of Higher Education, 2013.

Index